109

HANK HANEY'S
ESSENTIALS OF THE SWING

HANK HANEY'S
ESSENTIALS OF THE SWING

A 7-POINT PLAN FOR BUILDING A BETTER SWING AND SHAPING YOUR SHOTS

Hank Haney

WILEY

John Wiley & Sons, Inc.

Published by John Wiley & Sons, Inc., Hoboken, New Jersey
Published simultaneously in Canada

For general information about our other products and services, please contact our Customer Care Department within the United States at (800) 762-2974, outside the United States at (317) 572-3993 or fax (317) 572-4002.

Wiley also publishes its books in a variety of electronic formats. Some content that appears in print may not be available in electronic books. For more information about Wiley products, visit our web site at www.wiley.com.

Library of Congress Cataloging-in-Publication Data:

Haney, Hank.
    [Essentials of the swing]
    Hank Haney's essentials of the swing : a 7-point plan for building a better swing and shaping your shots / Hank Haney.
        p.   cm.
    Includes index.
    ISBN 978-0-470-40748-6 (cloth)
1. Swing (Golf) I. Title. II. Title: Essentials of the swing.
  GV979.S9H279   2009
  796.352'3—dc22

                                                    2008036263

Printed in the United States of America

10 9 8 7 6 5 4 3 2 1

CONTENTS

FOREWORD

"May I tell you something?" Hank Haney asked. He's been watching me play golf for twenty years, exercising singular restraint in never once fixing what is so clearly a flawed action. Sam Snead once said my grip resembled a can of worms. The writer Charles Price once said that if I hit the ball any lower I'd be playing underground. The comedian Ray Romano once observed that my putter resembles a metal detector. But through all of these years, Hank suffered in silence.

He couldn't take it anymore on the 13th fairway at Pine Valley Golf Club, where we get together every spring for a couple of days of nonstop golf. On this occasion the catalyst was a weakly struck 3-wood that found the sandy hazard short and left of the green.

"Let me show you something," he said. "You play a shot by walking up to the ball and taking your stance and looking down at the target. For as long as golf's been played, no good golfer ever started from beside the ball. Golf starts by standing behind the ball and looking at the target. Then you walk to the side of that line and take your address position."

I guess he had a point. Why should I think I'd be the first "good golfer" in five hundred years to start my setup from beside the target line? There's a good chance that the coach of Tiger Woods may know something about how to set up to the ball, so I nodded knowingly and filed his advice away for future application. Since that revelation, I can't say it's exactly transformed everything. My trajectory is still practically underground, but sighting the target from behind the ball has given me more consistency. It has the secondary effect of improving my posture. And it forces me to slow down, which has always been a mental fault.

When I reported to Hank months later that his impromptu lesson made an impression on me, he said: "You could make an argument that everybody's swing mistakes come from setup mistakes. That doesn't mean they are all going to go away if you set up well, but the whole evolution of your swing might have started just from setting up poorly. I try to make my teaching as simple as I can. All I'm trying to do is help you take a little step. And then if you can take a little step, then you take another one. I don't want to make it more complicated by advocating giant leaps. Just be patient with a little step. If you take enough little steps, you are going to cover a tremendous amount of ground.

"The hard part as a teacher, though, isn't necessarily looking at somebody and seeing what they need to do, but it's the convincing part. In your case, what struck home was my statement about five hundred years, as long as golf's been played, nobody has ever started from the side and played well. So that was the convincing part that got you to commit. It was the most important part of the message for starters, because if it didn't come with that, it wouldn't have clicked."

"So what's the next step?" I asked.

"What are you looking at when you now start the swing from behind the ball?" replied Hank. "Pick an intermediate target—a leaf, a sprig of grass, a spot on the ground—and set your aim to that point. You know, Nicklaus and Tiger both pick that intermediate target right out in front of them. In effect, bringing the target closer. And, my gosh, it's just amazing that those two guys do something that simple and yet everybody else who plays golf doesn't do it. You know, I mean, what else do you need? People want to make the game harder than it is. My teaching is about making it simple."

Over many hours of discussion through the years, Hank has convinced me that there are two legitimate ways of teaching. The first is a quick fix. In golf, the master of the quick fix is the British genius John Jacobs, who's considered the godfather of the European Tour and is one of Hank's original mentors. Jacobs could stand with his back to the student, observing only the flight of the ball, and magically offer the key setup changes necessary for improvement. "Basically when you do that, you're picking which bad impact you're going to live with," says Haney. "In other words, you might make somebody whose swing is too steep swing more shallow. Now they are on their way to being too shallow, but that's a lot better than being too steep. Sometimes Jacobs strengthens the grip—rotates the hands clockwise on the club—and once again fixes the problem by turning a slice into a hook.

"You've got to have some element of that in your teaching, or you're never going to be successful, because it's what everybody wants. Even students who say they don't want it, want it, because everyone's determination and persistence and dedication to a swing change is going to be tested at some point. You can line up somebody with a good grip and all the fundamentals, but if they're hitting grounders trying to make the change, how long will they stick with it?"

Haney believes the other method is to teach swing shape. The theory is, if you create a great-looking swing, you'll get a great-looking shot. "Every teacher I know, regardless of what they say about 'teaching the student, not the swing,' actually teaches a swing based on a model," says Haney. "Even the biggest proponent of 'I work with what you've got and I don't change it all around' still has some vision of what the swing should look like."

Hank's first two books were constructed around the first way to teach—fixing swing problems—and they really offered insight into the way he gives a lesson. If you've read those books, and for those who haven't I recommend you do, you would walk away having a pretty good idea of what taking a lesson from Hank would be like. In this book, Haney and his talented collaborator, *Golf Digest*'s European correspondent John Huggan, explain Hank's vision of what every aspect of the swing should look like. He's focused more on everything you would do, piece by piece, to build the best swing that you could for you. There's no short game, no putting—just full swing. *Hank Haney's Essentials of the Swing* is a culmination of thirty years of teaching. It's the model on which Hank bases his philosophy of the game. It's everything he now pours into the young students at the Hank Haney International Junior Golf Academy, and it's everything he's imparted to Tiger Woods over their five years of work together.

"Tiger's thirst to improve is greater than anybody I've ever seen," says Haney. "Even though he's achieved so much, it's not something he ever talks about, or thinks about, or dwells on. Everybody talks about what Tiger wants to do—like he wants to beat Nicklaus's record, win the most majors, set records. I love when I hear everybody say that, because in all the time that I have spent around Tiger I've never heard him, one time, say anything like that. The only goal I've ever heard him talk about is, he wants to get better. And I know the way he thinks. He thinks, 'If I get better, everything will take care of itself—all those other things will just be a foregone conclusion.' So yes, he's achieved so much, but he doesn't act like he has. He just acts like it's all ahead of him, and what excites him is the opportunity to improve."

When Tiger took his hiatus from the game in 2008, he called Haney on his cell phone the day before his knee surgery with one question: "What's the plan going to be for when I get back?"

"But you're not going to be back for eight months," replied Hank.

"Yeah, but I want to be thinking about what we need to work on."

As an observer of both Tiger and Hank, I sense it's this quality that binds them together and provides the challenge for both to keep going. *Hank Haney's Essentials of the Swing* offers an insight into the best thinking about the golf swing and how to apply it to your own game. It's all about getting better. If you're driven to improve, if you're willing to be patient and take one step at a time, this book is the journey of a lifetime.

Jerry Tarde
Chairman and Editor-in-Chief, *Golf Digest*

ACKNOWLEDGMENTS

For everyone who has ever taught, regardless of the subject matter, there has always been someone who in turn showed him or her the way. For me it was Jim Hardy. I was a freshman on the University of Tulsa golf team in 1974, the year I met Jim. He was the new pro at the club where my parents belonged, the Exmoor Country Club in Highland Park, Illinois. I was struggling with my game and heard that Jim was a great teacher; he had been an All-American at Oklahoma State and played on the PGA Tour for ten years. So I drove home for the weekend—a twelve-hour trip—to meet Jim, hopeful that he might take a look at my swing. It was early in March and the course wasn't even open yet, so I brought my own shag bag.

When I went into the pro shop that Saturday morning, Jim and his new assistants were setting up the shop for their first season and I introduced myself. When Jim asked me what I was doing in town, I told him I was struggling with my game and had come home to practice for the weekend. Jim said he would come out and watch me if he got a chance. Sure enough, about an hour later he appeared. It was the first real golf lesson I had ever had. Jim didn't just watch me hit a few balls; he stood out there with me for six hours. I think that was the day I decided to become a golf instructor.

Most people who are successful at something have someone who inspires them, and Jim inspired me to teach golf. It wasn't just his incredible knowledge of the game of golf that impressed me, but the fact that he cared so much. To stay out there for so long with someone he had just met was impressive, especially as the temperature never got above thirty-two degrees. I guess I showed Jim my desire on that cold day. But he showed me more than anything else what it takes to be a great teacher—a passion for helping people. Jim went on to be a huge influence on my career. Not only did he teach me about the golf swing, but he also showed me what it took to be a top teacher. I know that Jim is proud of what I have done in my career and I can only hope that along the way I have been as helpful to other teachers and especially my students as he was to me.

For over twenty years I have been associated with *Golf Digest* magazine, and for over twenty years John Huggan has been my writer, first with my articles in the magazine and then with my golf instructional books. It sure has been easy working with John; he is highly knowledgeable about the golf swing and understands how I think in terms of teaching the game. John has been a great friend and a great supporter of mine. In fact, when I first stared teaching Tiger Woods and it seemed that everyone in the media was doubting my instruction, it was John who said give Hank a chance and Tiger will be better than he has ever been. Everyone needs support and friendship, and John has always been there for me.

Thanks also to my partner at Hank Haney Golf, Steve Johnson. You have always been there for me, pushing me, challenging me, encouraging me, and supporting me. I appreciate your help with this book.

I also appreciate the help of my photographer, Dom Furore. Dom is a great friend and has been helping me with my books and my *Golf Digest* articles for over twenty years; he always does an incredible job. I also want to thank Lukas McNair, a member of my teaching staff in Dallas, for his help with the pictures. And to Scott Addison, thanks for your great work on transforming the pictures that Dom took into the great drawings in this book.

A special word of thanks goes to Stephen S. Power, who edited the manuscript and whose suggestions were so helpful. And a thank-you to my agent with Octagon, Jeremy Aisenberg, for his help in lining up a great publisher in John Wiley & Sons.

Finally, I want to thank all of the great students I have had over the years. I always have said that in order to be a great teacher, you have to have great students, and I was lucky in that regard. To Mark O'Meara and Tiger Woods, thanks; you guys have made me look like I knew what I was talking about.

INTRODUCTION

This book is going to make you a better teacher of yourself and in turn a better golfer.

When you teach golf, there are two ways you can approach things. You can work from the ball flight, then back to the ball. In other words, you identify a ball-flight error, analyze what causes it to happen, and then work on correcting it. There's some of that in all teaching, as an improvement in the way the ball is flying gives the student instant feedback on what he is working on. On the other hand, there are those who label such a method of teaching as no more than a short-term, Band-Aid approach. It is, after all, easy to change someone's ball flight through a minor alteration in grip, stance, or ball position.

The other approach to teaching and learning is through working on the shape of your swing and your fundamentals. The idea is that if you make a great swing, you will hit a great shot.

As a young man, I was an avid reader of golf instruction books. The one that had the most influence on me was Ben Hogan's *Five Lessons: The Modern Fundamentals of Golf*. I read it over and over. But the funny part was, I never really knew what was in Ben Hogan's book until after I had figured things out for myself. I think this book is one that you, too, will read over and over again and find a better understanding of something every time you do.

Another one of my favorite books was *Practical Golf* by John Jacobs. I worked for John early on in my teaching career, and he is the teacher who most influenced me. He is, in my mind, the greatest teacher the game of golf has ever known. What I learned mostly from John was a systematic way of analyzing the most important thing in golf, ball flight. I remember one of the first golf classes I ever did with John. It was in Florida. He started the class—there were thirty people in it—by picking out one person. He would have that person hit while John stood with his back to the student, looking down the range. After watching the ball's flight, its trajectory and curvature, he would call one of his assistants over and tell them to change this, this, and this, then have the pupil hit another shot. Sure enough, the shape and trajectory of the shots improved.

So ball flight can be your best teacher if you pay attention to it and understand it. John Jacobs illustrated that perfectly. Look at the ball flight. Identify the ball flight. Figure out what is happening at impact to cause that flight. Then figure out which fundamental you need to change in order to change that impact and, in turn, the ball flight.

If you understand the fundamentals of the golf swing and apply them to ball-flight principles, things become clearer to you as you learn to be a better golfer. But, like me, you will have to work it out for yourself.

That's the way it is with all students, to be honest. I try to help all of my students figure things out for themselves. You never really "own" the knowledge until you have gone through that process. And that holds true for every one of my students over the years, even Tiger Woods. As I work with the man who in my opinion is the best golfer who ever lived, I see my role as helping him figure things out for himself. Until he does that, he, like everyone else, doesn't really understand what he is trying to do.

When you take a lesson from me—or read this book—I want you to walk away with that understanding. I don't want it to be, "Well, Hank said to do this and Hank said to do that." That's only half the battle. Blindly following instruction isn't going to give you the understanding you need to be the best golfer you can be. Remembering the last thing your instructor told you to do is not really learning. This book is about making you the best player you can be. The essence of true learning is gaining an understanding of the subject for yourself.

There's a big difference between learning and merely memorizing what someone tells you, just as there is a big difference between mindlessly hitting shots on the range and actually working on what you are trying to achieve with your swing.

In learning golf, I looked at all the ideas and theories as I grew up in the game. Through that process, I began to come to my own conclusions. And as I did that, my understanding grew. I was like that with Hogan's book. Right away I knew I liked what he was saying. But I didn't really understand it. Not at first.

Later, when I worked for John Jacobs, I learned a different philosophy based on the flight of the golf ball. John was a genius when it came to quickly and accurately diagnosing swing problems, so his emphasis was on getting students to make quick corrections to whatever ball flight they were struggling with. It was also a great learning experience for me. Every golf swing has good aspects to it, but equally, within every swing there are mistakes. If you have an even number of mistakes—each one canceling out another—you can hit good shots and play good golf. But the closer your number of mistakes is to zero, the more consistent you are likely to be.

There's a danger in that line of thinking, though. It can easily lead to a swing that is full of compensations. In other words, if your shots are tending to finish, say, to the right of where you want them, one way of fixing that might be to turn your hands to the right on the club, thereby strengthening your grip. Or you may be hitting your shots "fat," with the club contacting the ground just behind the ball. A simple fix for that is just moving the ball back in your stance a little.

All of that is easy, natural, and human nature; we all want a quick fix—and there are plenty of those in these pages—so that we can get out on the course and enjoy playing. But what happens is that, over time, you end up doing exactly what you are trying not to do in your swing. You are building a method on mistakes, one piled on top of the other.

Yes, you may hit better shots for a short time, but you will never be consistent. When you have one mistake compensating for another mistake, it is hard to make the same swing over and over. Plus, there will always be "holes" in your game. Where you may be more than competent off, say, an uphill lie, you won't be nearly as good off downhill lies.

For the same reason, anyone with something of an unorthodox style is always going to have shots that, at the least, they struggle with. Actually, the reality is that such a golfer is going to have shots that he just can't play at all.

Let's say you are having trouble with a slice. Strengthening your grip will help you with that banana ball, but the result is that the clubface is going to be a little closed at the start of your swing, which will have an adverse effect on your pitching and chipping.

Or let's say you move the ball back in your stance so that you can hit shots more solidly—which you will. But suddenly you are tending to push the ball to the right of your target. So you aim left a bit more. Then a slice creeps in. So you aim left even more. And so on. Each mistake leads inevitably and inexorably to another.

In other words, those little corrections are great for getting through the next hole or round, but they aren't going to make you a better player.

Still, if I'm honest, that system of "quick fixes" worked well for me as a teacher. I had a lot of success helping students, although it was a transitory success. It was never long before most of them were back with their new and latest problem. But, as I say, it worked well, especially in a golf school environment where teacher and pupil have a limited amount of time together.

That's true of every lesson, actually. For one thing, most people have a limited attention span. Boredom sets in. And for another, very few students are in good enough physical shape to stand there and beat balls for hours on end. They get tired. Moreover, not many students are patient enough to work through a period of failure in order to build a better swing. Few people want to hear how much their swing has improved when they are not yet hitting the ball any better.

Those three factors all work against any kind of long-term process. But earlier in my career, I didn't have that luxury. I was a fixer of mistakes, an adjuster of mistakes, and, sometimes, an adder of mistakes.

As you can imagine, I eventually became dissatisfied with that approach to helping my students. All I was doing was applying Band-Aids to their multitude of problems. That was ultimately not what I wanted to do: my desire was to cure their problems, not just hide them.

Without getting too dramatic about things, I had a vision in my mind. I could "see" the correct swing, and that is what I wanted to teach to every student. It was never going to be a quick process, of course, but rather a case of building toward the perfect swing. This is the Holy Grail for every golfer. If you make a perfect swing, you will hit a perfect shot. That is basically what this book is about.

A big part of what I see as a correct swing is the plane of that swing. Hogan had a great image in his book, where he had an imaginary pane of glass angled from his shoulders down through the ball. But although it was a great image, I came to the conclusion that ultimately it didn't make sense, as no golfer sets up on that plane to begin with.

As I thought more and more about the golf swing, I realized that the golf club is not swung on a single plane. It is just about physically impossible. Rather, the golf club is swung on many planes that all have the same plane angle. So what is the correct plane angle? The plane angle that really matters is the one at impact. And that is the one you want to create at address between the ground and your club. You want to swing the club up and down on planes that are the same angle as the plane of the club at address. It has never made any sense to me to create one angle at address, then swing on and ultimately return to another angle at impact.

So while there are many planes in your swing, there must be

only the one plane angle. And that is the image I always want you to have in your mind as you swing. Think about what the golf club is doing. Its path is essentially your swing plane. Everything you do in your swing is in order to achieve the correct plane. It's that important.

You set up to the ball in order to create a certain plane. You grip the club in a way that will help you create that same plane. You turn your body in the way that best creates that plane. Everything you do in the swing—with your hands, arms, and body—is designed to get the club swinging on the correct plane.

When you hit different types of shots, such as fades or draws, you simply tilt that same plane in different directions. But it is still your swing plane. When you change the trajectory of your shot, you use the same swing plane; mostly what varies is the length and speed of your swing.

All of which is why, whenever I give a lesson, I always have an idea in my mind of just what that pupil's model swing will look like. And I know how to get them to that point. I call that having a plan that goes from A to Z. Z is always the same thing. You can't get to Z without knowing where A, B, C, D, and all the rest are. I mean, how are you going to know where the club should be at the top of your backswing if you don't know how to start it back, away from the ball at address? And how are you, without a picture of the follow-through in your mind, going to know how to start the club down from the top? That's like trying to aim when you don't know where your target is.

Z is the perfect swing, perfectly neutral and devoid of compensations or mistakes. With the perfect swing you can hit any kind of shot. You can hit it high; you can hit it low. You can hit it right to left; you can hit it left to right. You can control the shape and trajectory of your shots with a powerful, repeating method.

As your swing improves, you'll also get better at seeing and feeling what is still wrong with it, which will enable you to correct it further. The curse of the good golfer is knowing that you could be better, but the joy of golf is striving to achieve that improvement. The perfect swing is the one we are chasing.

Think about it. Over the course of a year Tiger has days when he can hit any shot perfectly. But he also has days when he struggles with one shot or another. He's human like the rest of us. But he has gotten closer to perfection than anyone. He has tasted that perfection and he wants more of it. In the end he wants to truly own his swing. That is why he works so hard. And that is why, if you want to improve, you will have to work hard, too.

1 THE PLAN

To build your swing,
you are going to need a plan.
This is where I come in. My starting
point, as it was when I worked under John
Jacobs, is your ball flight. I need to capture your
attention; I need you to have confidence in what I am
saying.

I can achieve both of those things right off the bat by giving you a better ball flight and by creating the first picture of just what your swing should look like. That's why a lot of teachers use video and pictures when diagnosing and explaining where students need to go and be in their swings. They are trying to create a visual image in the student's mind.

You as a student have some decisions to make. If your aim is to be the best golfer you can be, then your program for improvement is simple: start at A and keep working until you get to Z.

In order to improve you need to have a plan, one that goes from A to Z. And, so that you can figure out what B, C, D, E, and so on are, you need to know what Z is. You need a picture of your end result in your mind if you are going to work your way in that direction.

Having a plan is the approach that I have always taken with my students, no matter how good the student is to begin with. I remember the first time I set eyes on Mark O'Meara. He didn't have a plan. I was a young teaching professional at Pinehurst in 1980 and he was in his second year on the PGA Tour struggling to keep his card. When he arrived at the Hall of Fame Classic, he was 124th on the money list and badly in need of a good week. He had made something like $28,000, he had just missed the cut, and there were only three more tournaments left on the schedule.

Mark had won the U.S. Amateur Championship and been Rookie of the Year on the PGA Tour the year before but had never taken a golf lesson in his life. He got by on natural ability and a smooth rhythm. Amazingly, he didn't know much of anything about the swing or even his own swing. When he got to hitting it bad, his prescribed remedy was invariably to slow his swing down. Every bad shot, in his mind, came from swinging too fast.

Anyway, he was on the driving range at Pinehurst when I appeared. He was hitting this big duck hook. I watched him hit for maybe ten minutes, during which time I never said a word. In my mind I was running through all the steps he needed to take if he was ever going to get his swing back on track. Not only that, I was formulating a plan for explaining the plan.

He didn't know any of that, of course, and eventually he asked me what I thought. I suggested we go inside for a little while and have a drink and a chat. His reaction was that he didn't have time; he was out there grinding to save his tour card. I understood that, but if he was serious about getting better, he had to know what it was he needed to do. I knew this would be a big decision for him, so it required an explanation from me.

So we went inside and talked for thirty minutes, during which time I told him everything I thought he needed to do in his golf swing if he wanted to be the best that he could be. When I was finished, I asked him if he was prepared to make the necessary commitment. I had a pretty long list of changes to make, changes he would find difficult in the short term.

Change is like that for every golfer. It is uncomfortable. But he wanted to do it. So that weekend we started working. I told him where Z was and what every letter in between represented. And, as it turned out, he made the last three cuts of the year on the PGA

Tour and won enough money to keep his tour card for the next year.

That next year he worked really hard on his plan. We both did. And he got a little better. By the end of 1981, he was progressing with our plan nicely. In 1982, he had fifteen top-ten finishes and was second on the money list. All because he had a plan, was committed to it, and followed it through.

The approach I had used with Mark O'Meara came into play again almost twenty-five years later. When Tiger Woods called me in March 2004 and asked me to help him with his golf game, I had two reactions. One, this was the opportunity of a lifetime to work with the greatest player in history. And two, I was happy because I already had a plan in mind for his swing. In fact, I have a plan in my mind for every golf swing I have ever seen.

Like Mark, one of the first things Tiger asked was what I thought of his game. In the understatement of all time, I told him I thought it was great and that he was obviously working on a lot of good things. That went without saying. I had watched him from afar and had always been impressed. Who wouldn't be?

But I told him that it was difficult for me to work out in my mind what his plan was. I wasn't really sure that he had a good plan, one that would allow him to keep improving, to be the best that he possibly could. So I told him that the first thing we needed was that plan. Once we had that, we would know where we were headed, step by step.

Since then, Tiger has worked hard. He always has a plan every day that he goes to the golf course, whether it is to play or to practice. And he has always stuck to his plan. I think that is one reason he has improved every year we have worked together. All it takes is having a plan and working the plan, and Tiger knows this better than anybody.

The problem with having a strict plan, of course, is that, within that process, you still want to play golf, maybe compete in tournaments, and at least enjoy being out on the course with your buddies.

So a temporary adjustment may be called for. You have to build a powerful and repeating swing through solid fundamentals, but it's okay to patch things up now and then as you go through the process.

For example, it's okay to, say, strengthen your grip in order to hit better shots in the short term. Here's the key, though. At the same time you must continue to work on the fundamentals—the building blocks, the essentials if you will—of your perfect swing. If you do that, a strong grip will eventually cause you to start hooking the ball to the left. At which time you will want to move your hands back into a more orthodox position on the club. So, in the end, you will get to where you want to be.

Be aware that, at any stage in this whole process, I don't want you to feel that your goal of having a correct golf swing is an impossible dream. Regular doses of positive feedback are vital if you are to stay committed. Those can come from two areas. You can look at your swing and see that it is getting better. Or you can look at an equivalent improvement in your shots. You won't be surprised to hear that the one that carries the most weight is the latter! Knowing your swing is getting better can be a tough sell for even the most committed student if he is continuing to hit ground balls.

Still, this isn't as daunting as it sounds. Within the process of improvement, you are always going to be working on certain fundamentals of the swing. They are not that complicated. Part of my time during every lesson is spent focusing on ball flight; the rest I'm thinking more of long-term correction of faults. All of which will help you make the powerful, repeating swing that can hit every kind and shape of shot—with every club in your bag—with equal ease on a consistent basis. That's our goal. Let's go get it.

Here's how you make your plan. Start by analyzing your ball flight. In particular, what are your critical ball-flight mistakes? Do you have a tendency to slice the ball to the right or do you have a tendency to hook the ball to the left? The club that you want to look at the closest in determining your ball-flight curvature mistake is your driver. This is because the driver is the straightest-faced club in your bag and the most likely to curve. Also pay attention to the direction that your ball tends to start out; if it doesn't start straight, it can only start right or left. Then look at your middle irons and analyze the trajectory of your shots. Does the ball tend to fly too high, too low, or on the correct trajectory? Next, look at the solidity of your shots on the clubface; obviously this factor influences your distance the most. When you mishit shots, do you tend to hit them off the heel or the toe of the club? And do you tend to hit the ball too high or too low on the clubface if you don't make solid contact?

Once you have established what your ball-flight mistakes tend to be, you will have a clearer picture of where to look if your plan needs to be adjusted or revised or where you just need to focus more attention. Each player's plan for improvement will always involve working on the essentials of the golf swing. The essentials, or fundamentals as they are often referred to, that I take you through in this book are the keys to a powerful and repeating golf swing. Start with chapter 2 and work your way straight through the fundamentals and make sure you follow that routine every time you practice. No matter how well you think you have a fundamental mastered, you still need to recheck it every time you're out on the course. This is so important: never take anything for granted; keep rechecking and working on the essentials of the swing, and you will always keep improving.

2 THE GRIP

If you're like most golfers I meet, you probably think that the grip isn't the most interesting aspect of golf. Nor is it the most exciting subject on which to start any book. But here's the thing: as your only direct contact with the club, the grip is the most essential fundamental in any and every golf swing. Now, I also know you've probably heard that a million times in every instruction book and golf magazine you've ever read. But there is a reason for that: it's true (figure 1).

Here's why. To a greater extent than any other aspect of your swing, the clubface controls the direction in which the ball is going to fly. That doesn't mean that there aren't other factors, of course. The path of your swing, for example; the angle at which the club approaches the ball; your swing plane—all are important, but a change in any of them doesn't have the same effect on your shots as a shift in the clubface. And the clubface, to a large extent, is influenced by your grip. Even the slightest change in

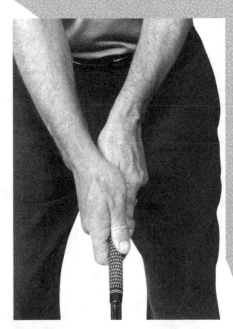

FIGURE 1 The grip is the primary control over the clubface. If you are going to build a great golf swing, your goal should be to have a totally neutral grip.

your grip can have a huge impact on the clubface at, well, impact. As a result, the importance of your grip cannot be overstated.

Still, despite everything I have just said, the grip is perhaps the most overlooked fundamental. I've watched thousands of golfers hitting balls, and I have to think that a very small percentage of them started each and every swing by thinking about their grip.

That's at least partly because the grip is perceived as dull and boring and repetitive. But that's something you must get past if you are to take the first steps on the road toward really improving your swing. Any golfer trying to improve would benefit from at least a little bit of a grip change, whether it is the positioning of the left or right hand, or the pressure you exert in each. There's a lot to your grip and so there are a lot of little things you can change in order to improve your swing and shots.

Let's say you are slicing your shots. One thing you can do to alleviate that problem is simply ease up on your grip pressure. By doing so, your hands will automatically become a little more active in your swing, which in turn encourages more of a right-to-left ball flight.

The opposite is also true. One cause of hooking is hands that are too active through impact. So you need to slow them down, which you can do just by holding on a little tighter, specifically with your right hand applying more pressure on top of your left thumb. The result is that your hands will work together more and eliminate the independent movement that is causing the hook you want to get rid of.

All in all, then, the grip is a lot more sophisticated and complicated than it first appears. Think about it. You have to put both hands on the club. Then you have to create a relationship between the two. That's where the questions begin:

Where do you put the club in your hands?

What sort of grip should you employ: overlapping or interlocking?

Which way are your hands turned?

How do you get both hands to work together?

How tightly should you hold on with both or either hand?

Are there any specific pressure points, and if so, where are they? Do they change during the swing or depending on the shot you want to hit?

That's a lot of questions for something that is supposed to be boring and one-dimensional!

The great thing to remember about your grip is that it is an easy thing to change in order to create a completely different feel in your swing. You're not swinging, you're not in motion, so it is something anyone, even someone with no athletic ability, can do. Your level of fitness or flexibility is largely irrelevant when it comes to creating a neutral grip. It is the one part of the swing that everyone should be able to get correct.

What makes it difficult, of course, is that any change feels uncomfortable, at least in the short term. And in my experience, people tend to equate that feeling to "incorrect." But that's rarely the case; most times it is "comfortable" that is incorrect. Which is the ironic thing about the grip, of course—nothing is both more uncomfortable and yet simpler to do. Changing your grip can be awkward and stress-inducing. But it also can be an investment in your future. If a grip change is what it takes for you to get better as a golfer, then the difficult times are worth battling through.

It's all about attitude, really. While others in the same position are wondering when, if ever, they are going to get comfortable with their new grip, take the view that it is only a matter of time before you do. Stay positive. Everyone struggles with changing his or her grip, even Tiger Woods.

Tiger and I began working together in March 2004. The 2004 Byron Nelson Classic was in Dallas in May. Tiger was leading after two rounds. He hadn't played particularly well, though, nor had he hit the ball that well. He was also in the middle of changing a few things in his swing, things that were improving but had hardly reached the "got it" stage. His results at that time showed that he was struggling with them a little bit.

I knew that one of the things that would really help him would be a little adjustment in his grip. Actually, it was a big adjustment. He had always held the club more in the fingers of the left hand, but I felt he would benefit by putting the club a little more in the palm of his left hand.

This was a big deal. Tiger at that time was already far and away the best player in the game and had gripped the club the same way his whole life. So I had to figure out a way to convince him that this was something to try. Tiger had made a comment to the press that he had listened to a lot of teachers in the past and 90 percent of what they said he didn't do. So I reminded him of that statement and asked him if he wouldn't mind trying something for a couple of shots, just to see what it felt like. Since he threw out 90 percent of what people suggested anyway, it shouldn't be a big deal to just try something. One thing about Tiger: he isn't scared to try to change; he is more scared to stay the same. He wants to improve. I really thought I had the way to at least get him to give this grip change idea a try. Sure enough, he said yes.

His first reaction was to say that he didn't know if he could even hit the ball. I just told him to hit one and see what happens. Then he said again, "I really don't know if I could even hit it with a grip like this." Well, I finally convinced him to hit one shot with that different grip and, sure enough, he hit a perfect shot. He looked at me and said, "Show me that grip again." So I did and the whole thing started again; he said, "I can't even believe I hit that ball." But he hit one more shot, and once again it was perfect. It felt awkward as he swung, but he could also feel how solid his impact became, how square the back of his left hand was to the target, and how much better his release through the ball felt. It was then that he turned to me and said, "We're going with this grip." And it has been that way ever since.

He had everything to lose—being the best player in the world—but was prepared to make a commitment to a change he thought would make him even better. The real key, however, is that Tiger doesn't put limitations on himself and didn't make this change into a bigger thing than it already was. Neither should you.

How to Hold the Club

This may seem obvious, but I can't tell you how often I have seen it ignored. The first key when taking hold of the club is to make sure you do it in such a way that the clubface is square. You must create that relationship between the clubface and the position of your hands. If that proves difficult for you to achieve, you can buy rubber grips with markings to show you exactly where each hand should go. Make it as easy as possible for yourself.

And another thing: although the proper grip is an alliance between two hands, I see a lot of people putting both on the club at the same time. Stop! This is a mistake. Look at so many of the leading professionals. Even at their stage of the game and level of play, they take great care when placing their hands on the club. It is one hand at a time for them (figure 2).

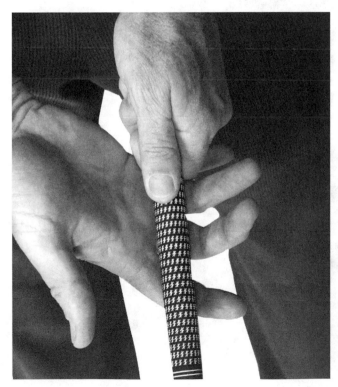

FIGURE 2 Take your grip slowly, one hand at a time, top hand first.

In fact, I would like to see you construct your correct grip with the clubhead held up and out in front of you so that you can see the clubface (figure 3). That way you can check that the clubface is square and at the same time that your grip pressure is appropriate. The right pressure is about the same as that you need to keep the club up in front of you.

FIGURE 3 Hold the club up off the ground when you take your grip.

Top Hand First

At this stage I'm going to assume that you are a right-handed golfer and so your top hand is your left hand.

The first thing you need to be aware of when positioning your left hand on the club is where the shaft is in relation to your palm. I see so many players holding the club too much in the fingers of the left hand, which leads to instability in the clubface (figure 4). Check it out for yourself. Holding a club in your left hand only, "milk" the clubface as you would when waggling before a shot. If you have the club too much in your fingers, you'll see a lot of wiggling in the clubface where the clubface is opening and closing. That's no way to be consistent.

Perhaps the only positive I can come up with for gripping the club in the fingers of your left hand is that it will give you a little more hand action and likely make it easier for you to close the clubface through impact. That's not bad if you are prone to slicing, but it's not the best way to grip the club if you want to hit the ball solidly and straight on a consistent basis.

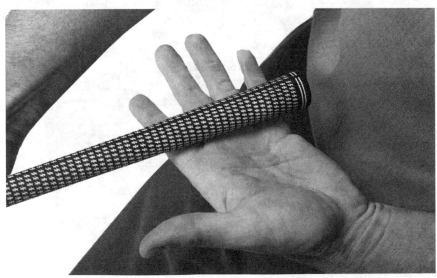

FIGURE 4 Gripping the club in the fingers of the left hand will make your clubface less stable through impact.

So here is where the shaft should be (figure 5). I like to see it angled more across the palm of the left hand than in the fingers. Let the shaft run from just under the pad of the hand through the first knuckle of your forefinger. When you close your hand, the thumb and the forefinger should press together to form a V shape. But, again, it should feel as if you are holding the club more in the palm than in the fingers.

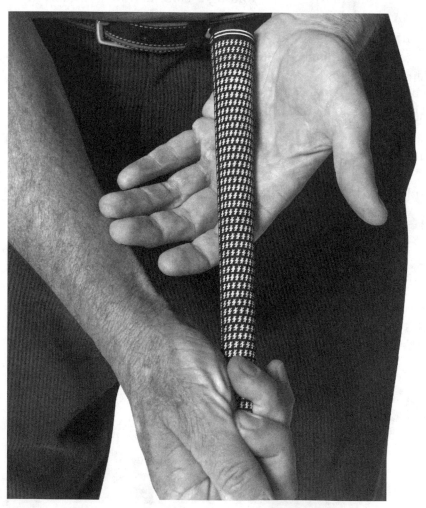

FIGURE 5 Angle the clubshaft across the palm of your left hand for the most stable grip.

A few checkpoints:

- Holding the club in your palm will produce what is known as a "short" left thumb on the shaft. If your thumb feels and looks extended, you are holding the club too much in your fingers. The thumb should be just to the right side of center on top of the grip.

- Form a "trigger" with your fore-finger under the shaft. That gives the club more support and encourages it to run correctly across the palm (figure 6).

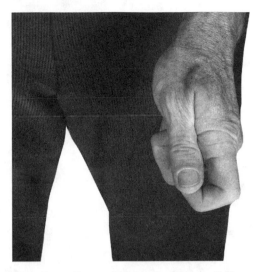

FIGURE 6 Form a "trigger" with your fore-finger and pinch your thumb and forefinger together to create a solid start to your grip.

As far as the knuckles on the back of your hand are concerned, you should be able to look down and see no more and no fewer than two knuckles. Three is too strong and will tend to produce a hook; one is too weak and will tend to produce a slice. Neutrality is what we are looking for here (figure 7).

Even after going through that list, take a look at your left-hand grip in a mirror. How many knuckles you can see has a lot to do with how and where you position your head. If you are one of those players who sets up with his head more behind the ball (farther from the target and too much toward your back foot) than is typical, then you are not going to see any knuckles. Equally, if your head is ahead of the ball (nearer the target and too much toward your front foot), you are going to see all of

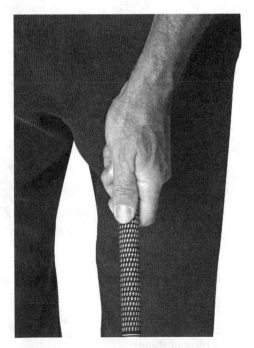

FIGURE 7 With a neutral grip you should see two knuckles when you look down.

your knuckles. So before you start counting knuckles, make sure your head is directly above your hands. Another checkpoint is that the V formed by your thumb and forefinger should be pointing between your right shoulder and right ear (figure 8).

FIGURE 8 Point the V formed by your thumb and forefinger just outside your right ear.

The Bottom Hand

I'm going to give you a choice here. You can either make what is known as an interlocking grip or go with its close relative, the overlapping grip. There is a third alternative in the so-called ten-finger grip, the hands unconnected, but I have never taught a student this grip, and it's largely obsolete these days and I wouldn't consider it.

The overlapping—or Vardon—grip is the most popular method (figure 9), but, on the other hand, the two greatest players of all time, Jack Nicklaus and Tiger Woods, both interlock (figure 10). Makes me wonder why anyone does anything else!

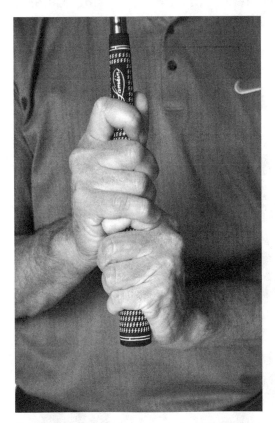

FIGURE 9 The Vardon, or overlapping, grip is a great option.

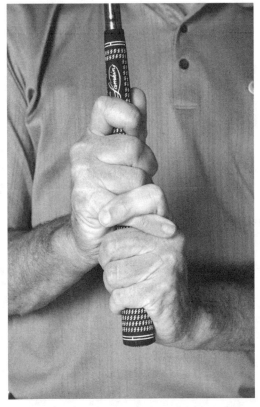

FIGURE 10 Jack Nicklaus and Tiger Woods both use the interlocking grip. What else do you need to know?

Actually, I know why the interlocking grip isn't as common as it maybe should be. I see an awful lot of players who do it badly. The tendency is, when interlocking the little finger of the right hand with the forefinger of the left, to go the whole way so that the fingers are fully entwined. If you do that, it is difficult to get the right hand out from under the club when you close it over the shaft. Try it and you'll see what I mean.

So when I say interlock, I mean interlock just enough so that the knuckles of those two fingers are touching, not so that they are jammed together all the way.

As for the overlapping grip, it is what it says it is: the little finger of your right hand sits on top of the forefinger of your left hand. The middle knuckle on your right little finger should sit right on top of the middle knuckle of your left hand. That

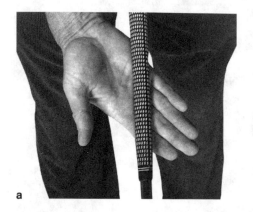

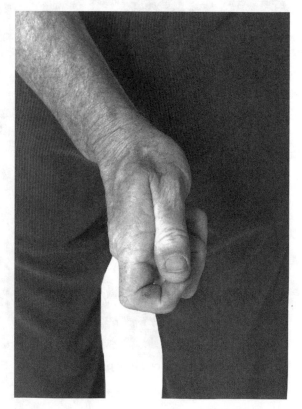

FIGURE 11 (a) The club should lie diagonally across the fingers and palm of your right hand. (b) Form a "trigger" with your right forefinger and pinch your thumb together with your forefinger, just like with your left hand. (c) In a good grip, your right hand always should hide your left thumb.

union will sit directly under the shaft of the club, lending support.

Whatever grip you choose to employ, when you place your right hand on the club, you want the shaft to run between the first and second knuckles of your right forefinger (figure 11a). Note, too, that your right hand/thumb should be a little "longer" than the left on the club. Make sure you form a "trigger" with your right forefinger, just like you did with your left forefinger (figure 11b). This will help keep the club stable at the top of your swing. You don't want your hands too close together. If they are squashed together, it will be as if you only have one hand on the club and your hands will restrict rather than encourage the proper release of the club. That's true of so many things in the grip, which, as I said right at the start of this chapter, is your main line of communication to the clubface (figure 11c).

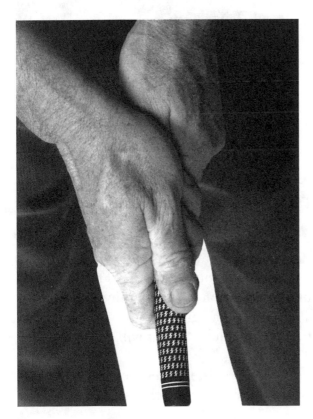

c

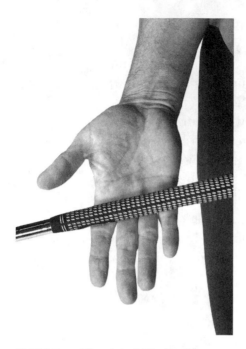

FIGURE 12 The clubshaft should run at an angle across the base of your fingers in the right hand.

When you close your right hand on top of the left, make sure that the shaft runs at a slight angle across the base of your fingers (figure 12). The key is not to hold on solely with the fingers, a mistake that matches the common error I see in many left-hand grips (figure 13). The hands should fit together snugly, the life-line on your right palm on top of your left thumb.

FIGURE 13 Gripping the club with the fingers of your right hand leads to instability and inconsistency in your clubface at impact.

Grip Pressure

I bet you have heard a lot about how your grip pressure should be light, as if you are holding a bird, which was an image associated with Sam Snead. Well, that's fine if you are a slicer of the ball looking to encourage more hand action in your swing in order to square the clubface at impact. But a light grip pressure isn't much use if you are prone to hooking, and in fact it will only make you hook worse.

For that reason, as so often in golf, I prefer the middle ground. I want your grip pressure to be not too tight nor not too light.

Which is another way of saying I'd be making that bird a little uncomfortable (figure 14)!

In my experience, better players tend to hold on to the club a little tighter than Sam recommended, and in some cases quite a bit tighter. The reason is that better players, as a rule, tend to fight a hook more than a slice. That firmness in the grip has the effect of enhancing a feeling of togetherness in the hands and, in turn, slows down the closing of the clubface through impact, thus reducing a player's tendency to hook the ball (figure 15).

Higher handicappers, in contrast, almost always hold the club way too tightly. This is partly the result of tension and apprehension over where the ball is headed, with the result being that those players who have too tight a grip have trouble squaring/ closing the clubface and are prone to slicing.

The bottom line? The ideal situation is that you hold on really tight with your fingers, but maintain a feeling of softness in your wrists, arms, and shoulders. In reality, that's impossible. But it's

FIGURE 14 Make sure the last three fingers of your left hand hold on to the club throughout the swing. Letting go at the top is a common problem.

FIGURE 15 Keeping your left thumb consistently pressed down on top of your right thumb is a good way to eliminate a hook.

not a bad thought to have in your head, in that it will tend to lighten your hold on the club and free up your upper body. That's where tension tends to accumulate, far more than in your hands.

If you set up tight and rigid, you have no chance of making a fluid, free-flowing swing.

As for specific pressure points within your grip, most of the pressure from both hands should come from above and underneath the shaft, not the sides. At address and throughout the swing, maintain pressure from above on your left thumb with the pad of your right palm. And do the same from underneath, pulling up

FIGURE 16 A neutral grip is a key factor in getting a square clubface at the top of your swing.

with your right forefinger. The right thumb, just so you know, is basically just resting on the club. There is no need to exert any pressure there, as is evident from the fact that great players like Fred Couples and Vijay Singh both have their right thumbs off the shaft at impact.

Just to be sure that your "pressure points" are in the right place, check both by "milking" the club. With your grip in place, ease up on the pressure, then regrip, ease up again, then regrip again. If you have a good grip, the clubface won't move.

In contrast, if you have the club too much in your fingers, controlling the clubface as you milk the shaft will be all but impossible. It will be all over the place, with the shaft twisting one way or the other. If you have a proper grip as we have described here, that won't happen. Any pressure will be exerted up and down on the shaft, not side to side.

Okay, now you have a neutral grip, one that will keep the clubface square to the plane of your perfect swing and square to your left wrist position from the start of your swing to the finish (figure 16). If the face and your left wrist do not match up, your grip is either too strong or too weak. And if that is the case, it is time to read this chapter one more time!

3 STANCE, POSTURE, AND ALIGNMENT

This part of the game involves very little, if any, physical movement—and so is often perceived as a little boring—but this chapter might just be the most important one in this book. If you don't get set up to the ball in a proper fashion, and if you don't create the proper angles at address, then your chances of making a correct and powerful swing are somewhere between slim and none. The good news is that you don't have to be special in any way in order to create a great setup.

Look at the backswing. For you, that is really the creation of a pivot. Part of that is creating a good coil in your swing, as you stay centered. In other words, you are coiling and turning around a certain axis. The image you want is of a rod going down through your spine into the ground and you rotating around that rod. If you don't define that axis properly before you swing, there is no way you are going to be able to turn around it. You won't stay centered. You won't have any chance to stay in your posture. And you won't build up a proper coil.

Let's get to achieving all three.

a

b

FIGURE 17 (a) Keep the clubface perpendicular to the target, and your feet, knees, and hips parallel to the left of the target line. (b) Set your arms, shoulders, and eye line parallel to the left of the target line, which is your intended line of flight.

Alignment

Here's something that is news to most golfers I meet. If you look at the most important part of your alignment, it would not be your feet. But it is relatively easy to first align your feet, then square your body and the club to the line along your toes that you have created. It is a good and easy reference point to what square to the target is (figure 17a).

So think of your feet as a starting point, nothing more. Then you can work through your knees, hips, arms, shoulders, and eyes, using the lines established by your feet and the clubface (figure 17b).

What is more interesting to note about foot alignment, however, is that it is far from an exact science. Three of the greatest ball strikers in the history of the game were Lee Trevino, Ben Hogan, and the famous—and eccentric!—Mo Norman. Norman always aimed a little to the right of where he wanted the ball to end up, then pulled the shot back onto that target. A slightly closed alignment will promote either a slight draw or pull. Trevino aimed well to the left and pushed everything. A slightly open alignment will promote either a slight fade or push. And Hogan was essentially square. In other words, in terms of alignment, the three men were all very different, yet all were magnificent shot makers.

Having said that, I like my students to be well coordinated so that everything is lined square if you are playing a straight shot. This means that your feet, knees, hips, arms, shoulders, and eyes are lined up parallel to the left of the target line—that is, what is considered square. And that starts with the feet. Think of your address position as being on a railroad track: your feet are on the inside rail and the clubhead and ball are on the outside rail. It's a familiar and well-used image in many instruction books. But it is so familiar for a reason: it works and is the simplest way of illustrating a square stance (figure 18).

FIGURE 18 Imagine you are lining up on a railroad track: your feet are on the inside rail and the clubhead and ball are on the outside rail.

Okay, time out for a second. During your golfing life, you may have read that the hardest shot in the game to hit is the perfectly straight one. So, following that premise, why is it that I want you to set up as if to hit the most difficult shot in the bag?

Well, first, I have never understood the argument that a straight shot is more difficult to hit than any other. Yes, it is easier to hit a slice or a hook in the sense that each slice is any shot that curves left to right or a draw is a shot that curves right to left. But how much does each curve? That is the really difficult part, controlling just how much spin you impart on the ball.

For that reason, it is my contention that it is not harder to hit a straight ball than it is to hit, say, a 9-yard draw. Or an 8-yard draw. Or a 10-yard fade. Slices and hooks are easy, if you don't have to say exactly how much the ball is moving in the air. The difficult part is being precise, whether the shot required is straight, a fade, or a draw.

Besides, if you are using the clubs and balls that are available on the market today, sidespin is being minimized by both, making the straight shot easier to produce than ever before. Brilliant scientists spend months trying to help you hit the ball straight, so why fight all that intellect? Line up squarely and in a neutral fashion. Go for the straight one as your basic shot and work from there!

Stance

Width is a much overlooked aspect of the stance. Once you are standing squarely to the ball, just how far apart should your feet be placed? And what does varying that width do to the position of the ball relative to your feet?

The first thing you need to do is let the length of the club dictate the width of your stance. The longer a club is, the wider your stance needs to be. But don't get carried away on either end of the scale. The difference between your narrowest and widest stances is only a few inches.

Let's start in the middle. If you are hitting a 6-iron, your feet should be shoulder width apart (figure 19). Imagine a line being drawn down from the outside of your shoulders; it should pass through the middle of your heels. Use this width of stance as a starting point for every other club.

Widening your stance has the effect of lowering your center of gravity and shifting the center of your body back, away from the target. At the same time, the ball effectively moves forward, toward the target, promoting more of a sweeping motion through impact. Being the straightest-faced club in your bag, the driver is best suited to that particular action, a fact accentuated by the ball being teed up off the ground (figure 20).

In contrast, a narrower stance with a shorter club automatically means that you will be standing closer to the ball (figure 21). This moves your body center forward, toward the target, thereby lifting

FIGURE 20 For a driver, the ball position should be just inside your left heel, with a slightly wider stance than with the irons.

FIGURE 19 For a 6-iron, the ball position should be just forward of center, with the stance not too wide and not too narrow.

FIGURE 21 For a wedge, the ball position should be a little farther back, and your feet should be just a little closer together.

your center of gravity and promoting more of a downward motion when hitting a short iron. As a result, a narrower stance will always tend to promote a slightly lower ball flight.

That's why the first thing to consider here is the length of the shot you are about to play. If you are faced with a relatively short shot and you have, say, a wedge in your hands, your right foot should be placed perpendicular to your target line, with your left foot both flared out something like 20 degrees and pulled back maybe an inch from square (figure 22). In other words, your feet should be slightly "open" (aligned to the left). This will help you turn your

FIGURE 22 Here the left foot is drawn back just a little to open the stance for a short iron.

left side through impact and into the follow-through. Turning through the ball more promotes a straighter shot and is a good way to eliminate a hook.

As the shot gets longer, your stance should get both "squarer" and wider. By the time you reach, say, a 6-iron, that line along your toes should be back to parallel with the target line, a relationship you want to maintain for every longer club and shot (figure 23). The only difference is that, as the shaft gets longer, your right foot should flare out just a little as your left foot flares out a little less.

FIGURE 23 With a middle iron, your stance should be dead square, parallel to the left of the target line.

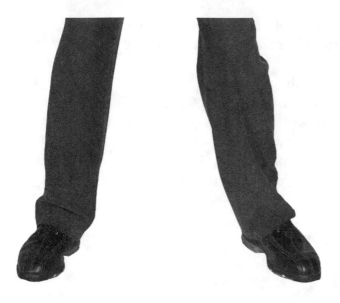

FIGURE 24 When using a driver, toe both feet out just a little to make it easier to turn both back and through.

When using the longest club in the bag, your driver, both feet should be turned out the same amount (figure 24). In order to maximize your hitting distance, you want to be able to turn your right side "out of the way" on the backswing. You want a feeling of being "behind" the ball at the top of your swing. Turning your right foot out will make this a little easier to achieve. This foot position will also tend to promote a little more of a draw shot rather than a fade.

To sum up, as your stance gets wider, it gets more square, with your right foot moving from square to toed out and your left moving from toed out to more square.

Ball Position

Much has been written about this aspect of the stance, but it is easy to get too bogged down in trying to be too exact with your ball position. Don't worry about it too much, at least initially. The ball will find its own place within your stance based on how you set the club down. If your arms are set in front of your body and the club-head is on the ground just as the manufacturer intended it to be, the ball will find that correct position.

For example, when you have a driver in your hands, the ball is going to be more forward, toward the target, than it would be for, say, a 6-iron (figure 25). Look at your driver. The face of the club is "ahead" of the shaft, so the ball has to follow suit and be slightly in front of your hands. In contrast, look at your wedge. If you just

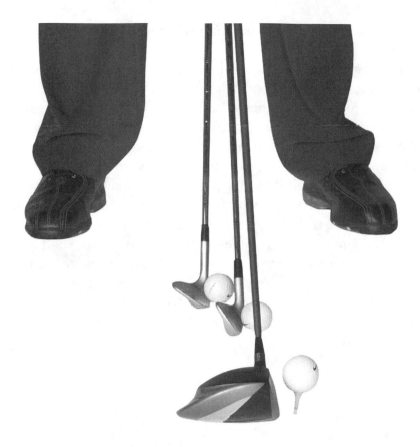

FIGURE 25 The ball position changes a little bit as your clubs get shorter, but it isn't more than a few inches for the whole set.

naturally address the ball, the ball position is going to be more back (away from the target) in your stance because the handle of the club is in front, nearer the target, than the clubhead. So, really, the correct ball position is built into the design of every set of clubs that is made, and it will vary slightly among the different clubs in your bag.

There are some parameters that you can go by when it comes to ball position, however. I like to see the ball pretty much opposite the left heel with the driver and fairway woods and moving back from there to the point where, for the wedge, it is just ahead of the middle of your stance. For any kind of "normal" shot, those are your limits.

Any incorrect ball position will have an adverse affect on your swing and subsequently your ball flight. If the ball is too far forward in your stance, a couple of things are likely to happen. First, you are going to contact the ball too late in the arc of your swing and you will tend to pull the ball. Second, you are going to be forced into swinging with too much of an upward motion into the ball. Equally, if the ball is too far back of your stance's center, you will inevitably make too much of a steep, downward hit and you will also have a tendency to push the ball.

Another consideration to take is how high you tee the ball with your driver. I must say that I am not a big fan of teeing up the ball too high. Again, that has an adverse effect on the motion you will make; you will tend to hit up on the ball too much. This will cause the bottom of your swing to be too far behind the ball. Tee up so that a little less than half of the ball is above the top of your driver (figure 26). That's enough for anyone.

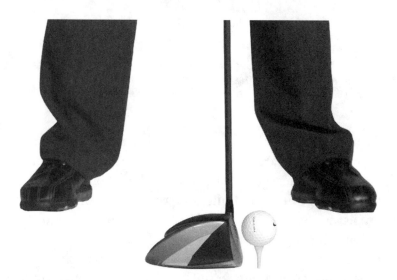

FIGURE 26 When teeing up the ball, less than half of the ball needs to be above the big clubheads of today.

Two things that hurt a lot of players' swings are the height of the tee and the length of the driver. Too many people seem to think that an excessively high tee and a long-shafted driver mean "power." This is true to an extent, but the long drive isn't the only shot you are going to need. What you gain in distance when you do happen to make a great swing and hit the ball solidly, you lose in consistency. So teeing the ball real high with a long-shafted driver is going to create a huge range in your shots. Your good ones will be great and your bad ones will be terrible. And it's my bet that you will produce more of the latter than the former.

One of the things that a long driver and high tee will do is make it hard for you to find the ball with the bottom of your swing—where you brush the turf while hitting the ball at the same time—and that is already one of the most difficult things for any golfer to do on a consistent basis. Show me someone who likes to tee the ball high and I will show you someone whose swing is too shallow coming into the ball.

Think about it. The longer your club is, the more of an arc you have to swing it on around your body. The bigger the arc, the longer your club is closer to the ground and the more things can go wrong, making a consistent bottom harder to achieve. The higher you tee the ball, the more you have to hit up. Any adjustment of that sort again makes it harder to find the bottom. Why make it harder for yourself than it already is?

The Clubface

There is only one exception to my "everything is square" rule at address, and that is the clubface. I like to see the face of the club ever so slightly open—aimed to the right—as it sits behind the ball (figure 27). Look at any number of leading players on tour, including Tiger Woods; they do exactly that.

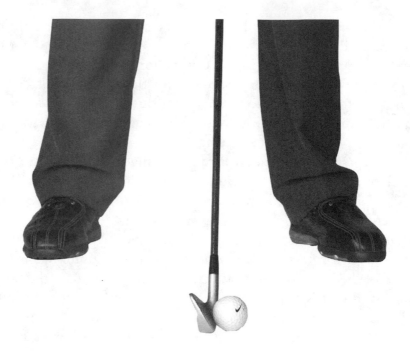

FIGURE 27 An ever so slightly open clubface is perfect when the clubhead sits behind the ball.

Which isn't to say that I don't want the clubface square at impact; I do. But think about it carefully. The club is a little behind the ball when you stand to the shot. So although you want to initially set the club down square to the target as a guide for your body, it isn't quite where you want it to be right before you take the club back. That's why, after you have assumed your stance, the face should then be set open just a little bit.

Actually, if your habit is to address the ball with the club an inch or so back from it, "a little open" has to be "a little bit more open." You don't want the clubface square an inch behind the ball on the downswing. If that happens, the club will have closed ever so slightly by the time it gets to the ball and you will hit the ball to the left. It's just logic, really. You actually set the club down at address in position so that it is square to the arc of your intended swing and not precisely square to the target.

Weight Distribution

Yet again, this is a very important yet much neglected aspect of the stance and your general posture. Where your weight is distributed on your feet has a follow-on effect on the plane of your swing.

All too often the root cause of a golfer swinging too much to the inside, or lifting the club up, or coming "over the top," is his weight distribution at address (figures 28a and b). If that is wrong at address, you can easily lose your balance, either back or forward, during the swing.

If any or all of this sounds like you, take a look at your weight at address. If you are like most people, your tendency will be to set up in a way opposite to your in-swing tendency. In other words, if you tend to fall backward onto your heels during your

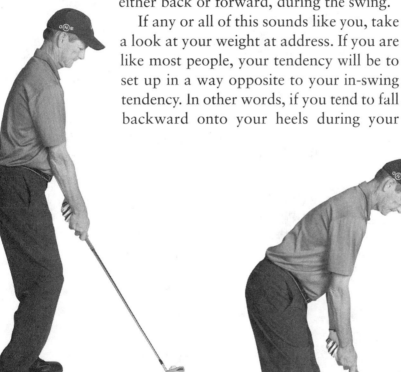

FIGURE 28 (a) Standing straight up and down with poor posture gives you nowhere to swing the club. (b) A bent-over posture with your weight back on your heels makes it next to impossible to swing the club on the correct swing plane and in balance.

FIGURE 29 Your weight should be evenly distributed on your feet. Starting on balance gives you your best chance to swing on balance.

swing, your weight will likely be too far forward, on your toes, at address. It's always a mistake to change your address position in an attempt to alter something that will happen during your swing. A perfect swing is made by building positive things on top of one another, not by compensating for one mistake with another. Never put mistakes on top of mistakes.

Think of it this way. If you set up with your weight in the middle of your feet and finish with your weight predominantly on your toes, don't compensate for that by changing your set-up position. Keep your weight evenly distributed and focus on maintaining your weight in the middle of your feet from start to finish. You can figure out what is causing you to fall forward later. Don't overreact by turning one mistake into two.

As a general rule, your weight should be neutral and even on your feet, not too far back on your heels, nor too far forward on your toes (figure 29). Most of your weight should be centered on the balls of your feet. In other words, you should be in an "athletic" position, as if you were about to shoot a free throw on the basketball court or field a ground ball in baseball. It's that simple.

Posture

From an erect starting point, with your arms right in front of you, bend a little from your hips, reach with your arms, then flex your knees a little (figure 30a). As you bend forward from the hips, your rear end should go out and up a little bit. Only then should you bend your knees. If you bend your knees first, your rear end will be pulled in.

Your knees should feel as if they are "knocked in" a little bit, with a little bit of tension apparent on the inside of both legs, all the way up from your ankles to your thighs. That builds the solid base that will later help you develop some coil in your swing.

As long as you maintain the relationship between your shoulders and your spine, that's a pretty good position right there, one that will work for every club in the bag (assuming your clubs are properly fitted in terms of lie and length to your physical characteristics); there is no need to change your posture from, say, driver to wedge (figures 30b and 30c). Where it is easy to get into trouble is when you start from a point where your upper body

b

a

c

FIGURE 30 (a) Good posture is essential to making a good swing. Bend slightly forward from your hips, keep a slight bend in your knees at address, and keep your weight on the balls of your feet. (b) Here is the correct posture with a driver, with just a slight bend in the knees. (c) Here is the correct posture with a short iron, with the arms hanging down from the shoulders.

is tilted one way or another, either toward or away from the target, or hunched forward, too much over the ball.

In passing, don't worry about how far the butt end of the club is from your leg when you address the ball. That distance is dependent on too many factors, the most significant being your own physical size. More reliable is to let your arms hang comfortably down directly below your shoulders (figure 31). Tension-free,

FIGURE 31 In a correct address position, your arms should hang free of tension underneath your shoulders.

they will find the correct spot by themselves. If you push your arms out too far, they will feel "heavy"; if they are too close to your body, you will feel "crowded." Let what feels right tell you what is right. The only way to get into the wrong place is by you distorting your body's natural tendencies.

Specifically, however, the triangle formed by your arms and shoulders is a key part of getting your arms positioned correctly in front of you (figure 32). If you distort that triangle, either by having your hands too far forward or too far back at address, then your perfect posture is going to be compromised. Your hands, by way of a reference point, should be directly in front of the zipper on your trousers. And your shoulders should feel as if they are pulling back a little bit. That will allow you to keep your upper arms close to your body during the swing. If your shoulders ease forward, your arms will become disconnected from your body. And remember, although you want a firm grip on the club, maintain softness in your wrists and arms.

Right Arm–Left Arm

I get asked a lot about the relationship between the arms and shoulders at address. And the answer is perfectly logical. Because the right hand is slightly lower on the club than the left, this must have an effect on the corresponding relationship between the shoulders.

Again, start from your erect position, the club held out in front of you. Bend forward from your hips. Because your right hand is the lower of the two, your right shoulder has to be the same amount lower than your left shoulder. It's just two or three inches lower, not six or seven (figure 33).

FIGURE 32 The triangle formed by your arms and shoulders should sit right in front of your body for all clubs.

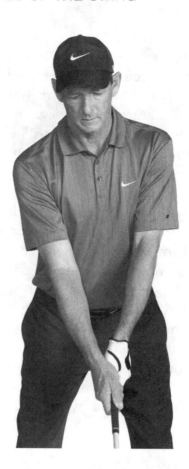

FIGURE 33 Your right shoulder should be just slightly lower than your left at address, the exact same amount that your right hand is lower than your left on your grip.

If your hands were together at the same height on the grip, your shoulders would be perfectly level and your arms parallel to the target line. And that, in fact, is a good starting point. From there, simply let your right hand slip down until you can comfortably form your grip. Your shoulder will follow your hand's lead.

Once you are in that address position, you want your left arm to be straight—but very definitely not stiff or rigid. My definition of straight is simply letting it hang by your side. That is as straight as it needs to be, at least at address. When you grip the club, your right hand is closer to the ball than your left hand. Your right elbow is slightly bent and your forearms should be perfectly parallel to the target line at address.

Keep Your Eyes Level

The alignment of your eyes at address has a big impact on the likely shape of your swing. If you set up with your eyes aligned to the right or left of where you want the ball to go, chances are your swing will follow that same path and this will promote a push and hook or a pull and slice. If you tilt your head—and therefore your eye line—one way or the other, you are more than likely to swing too flat or too steeply, with fat or thin shots being the result. So your eyes need to stay level to the ground and parallel to the target line (keep them focused right on the back of the ball if you are hitting a driver; more on top of the ball if have a short iron in your hands) (figure 34). Besides, if your eyes don't stay level during the

FIGURE 34 Focus your eyes level to the ground at address and keep them that way throughout the swing.

swing, it is harder to keep your balance. You won't have a perfect swing without perfect balance.

If you are having trouble with your eye level, wear a cap in practice and use the bill of it as a guide.

As a final check, your eyes are the last piece of our setup jigsaw puzzle. Everything should be aligned parallel to the target line (figure 35): your feet, your knees, your thighs, your hips, your arms, your shoulders, and your eyes. If I am looking at you from

FIGURE 35 Every part of your body should be parallel to the left of the target at address.

directly behind, down the target line, I shouldn't be able to see any part of the left side of your body. When you are in that position, you are perfectly set up, ready to create a positive reaction or swing.

One Last Thing

If you are going to get any part of your body alignment correct at address, make it your eyes and shoulders. They will have more of an effect on your impact and subsequently the flight of your shot than anything else, especially the path of your swing and the bottom of your swing arc.

If your eyes and shoulders are lined up too much to the right, you will almost inevitably take the club away too much to the inside on the backswing. If you do that, the club will almost certainly bottom out behind the ball, unless you come over the top of the swing—and then you have another set of problems. As an experiment, align your eyes and shoulders to the right at address and then try to take the club away outside the target line. Can't be done, can it?

4 THE BACKSWING

Okay, you are stand-
ing to the ball in the perfect
starting point for your perfect swing.
Your grip, your posture, your stance, your
alignment, your aim—everything is ready for you
to move the club into the backswing.

Hang on, though. If you're like every other golfer I
have seen, you will have a "trigger," a little move that is the
start of your backswing. It might be a little bouncing of the
club up and down. Some players turn their head to the right a
little. Others will kick their right knee in a little. Still others will
trigger their swing by pumping their grip a few times.

Take care, though. Don't overanalyze. Those sorts of moves are
mere mannerisms, unconscious movements that won't have any significant impact on the perfect position you have created at address. So there
is no real point in copying what someone else does. Mostly these little idio-
syncrasies are a waste of time and energy. Think about it. If you physically
mimic another player, you haven't really copied him at all; what was unconscious for him is conscious for you. So don't bother.

Even more important, the last thing you want to be doing is indulging in a
so-called forward press with your hands and the grip end of the club. All that
does is fundamentally change your setup and get you out of position, with your
hands suddenly too far forward and the club more than likely to move back too

much inside the proper line. Why go to all of the trouble of getting into a perfect position, only to go changing it at the last moment? It makes no sense. So don't do it.

The most important concept to understand in the backswing is that the golf club must swing inward and upward throughout the whole backswing. When you blend just the right amount of inward motion with just the right amount of upward motion, you will be swinging the club on the correct plane for you as an individual.

The First Move

To me, the backswing initiates more from the upper body than the legs. Think of your shoulders, your arms, and your hands as one unit, moving away from the ball together. As that happens, you want your lower body to resist, with your left heel staying as close to the ground as possible (figure 36). I'm not saying that it has to be flat on the ground. If you are not blessed with a great deal of flexibility, by all means let it come up a little, whatever you need to do to make a proper pivot. Take care, though. The danger in allowing your left heel to rise too much is that, as it does, everything else rises, too. So keep it to a minimum, no matter how much that minimum is for you. The less you move your lower body, the better.

FIGURE 36
Your lower body should resist moving as much as possible at the start of your swing.

Here's how it should feel. Your right leg should stay in place as the club moves back. And your left knee should kick in only a little. The more complete you can turn your upper body while you resist with your lower body, the better the coil you will develop (figure 37).

The idea is to get the club moving back on the correct plane, then "set" at the top—the club not only on the correct plane and in the correct position, but also your wrists properly hinged—all while your upper body coils around a resisting lower body (figure 38). The more you can do both, the more powerful your swing and shots are going to be.

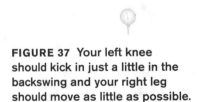

FIGURE 37 Your left knee should kick in just a little in the backswing and your right leg should move as little as possible.

FIGURE 38 Your hips ideally turn only half as much as your shoulders.

How well you can achieve that position depends a great deal on your physical condition and natural suppleness. The more you can turn your shoulders while resisting with your hips, the better you will be. The ideal, of course, is that you achieve a full shoulder turn with only half as much hip turn. And take care. Your hips must follow—not lead—the shoulder turn. But don't neglect your hips, either. Some hip movement is required to get the club all the way to the top of the swing. Think of moving your hips as you wind up on the way back, all so that you can unwind again on the way down.

In order to create the proper resistance going back, I like to see both feet firmly planted on the ground as the upper body turns (figure 39). Your weight should be on the inside of your right foot, your leg holding the position you created at address as you rotate around your right leg.

As you turn back, behind the ball, your left foot/heel should lift only a little, with the heel staying as close to the ground as is physically possible for you (figure 40). All of this is happening as the upper body is turning.

The big key in the takeaway, however, is the club and how it is moving into the backswing. For me, by the way, the takeaway ends when the

FIGURE 39 Practice turning with a club against your right leg to get the correct feel of turning around your right leg and keeping the weight on the inside of your right foot.

FIGURE 40 Lifting your left heel off the ground in the backswing is not a good idea.

shaft of the club is parallel to the ground. And it is, by far, the most important part of your swing, other than impact. While the perfect setup gives you a chance to make the perfect swing, the perfect takeaway is an absolute prerequisite. If you start wrong, you are going to have to compensate or recover later—none of which sounds like perfection—and your chances of hitting the shot you want will be hugely diminished (figure 41). Sure, you may get lucky now and then and find the middle of the clubface, but you are certainly not going to be consistent. Making compensations the same way time after time is just too hard.

FIGURE 41 Taking the club back too much to the inside and underneath the plane in the takeaway like this is the most common mistake amateurs make.

Take it from me: a faulty takeaway is going to leave you with holes in your game. You may find that you are fine with a driver in your hands, but not so good with the short irons. Or vice versa. You may find that hitting off a lie where the ball is below your feet isn't a problem, but that a ball sitting above your feet leads to all kinds of difficulties. Or it may be that you struggle from sand. There is always going to be a problem somewhere.

And those problems might not always be in your long game. A lot of times when I see a player with a faulty takeaway, he has a problem with his short shots. Pitching and chipping are areas of the game where you are using something less than a full swing. So it becomes even more important to get the takeaway right. On a shorter swing you have even less time to recover.

So although this book is focused on the full swing, think of this section as something of a lesson in the short game. The takeaway is that important; it sets up the whole swing, short or long.

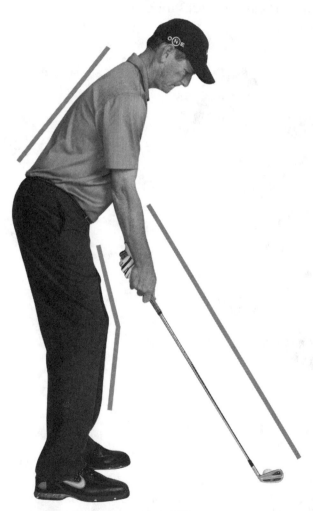

FIGURE 42 The correct swing plane angle is dictated by the angle of the clubshaft at address.

On Plane

Your aim, then, is to swing the club on the correct plane throughout. To achieve an on-plane swing, you have to start on plane. And that plane is created by the correct angle of the clubshaft at address (figure 42).

From address, swing the club back along the angle of the shaft (figure 43a). Don't go outside that angle, or inside it (figures 43b and c). Your aim is to stay on it, assuming you are attempting to hit a basic straight shot.

When you swing the club back, a few things start to happen. Your shoulders turn. You maintain the posture created at address. And your arms start the clubhead back from the ball.

Figure 43 (a) Here the club is right on plane on the takeaway, right along the original angle of the shaft. (b) Here the club is too much outside on the takeaway. (c) Here the club is too much inside on the takeaway.

Now, I can hear you ask, what does that feel like? When you are turning, your left shoulder is going to move down slightly and your right shoulder up a little, because you are bent forward from your hips. So you don't turn your shoulders exactly level; there is an angle there, the same angle you set up at address. There should also be a feeling of staying centered. You don't want to lean or sway forward or back, either of which will fatally alter your posture (figures 44a–d).

Figure 44 (a) Your shoulders should rotate 90 degrees to your spine angle. (b) Reverse pivoting like this is one of the worst mistakes a player can make. (c) Failing to rotate around your axis makes it hard to find your way back to the ball. (d) Rotating around your center axis is the most efficient and consistent way to swing a golf club.

a

b

c

d

When you make a correct turn, it should feel as if you are not using up a lot of space. You are staying in position, making what I like to call a "tight turn." The tighter and more efficient that turn is, the better your swing is going to be (figure 45). Think "centered" and "posture."

FIGURE 45 Keeping your eyes level to the ground as you turn is a big key to making a correct turn.

Think of it this way. Imagine a figure skater spinning. He or she stays beautifully centered and in his or her posture. If not, the skater travels across the ice and the spin never gains speed. A spinning top is another great mental image. When the top slows down, it starts to wobble. That is the equivalent of a golfer losing his posture and failing to turn on his proper axis. If you do that, you will never turn as efficiently, consistently, or quickly as you would if you retain your posture and turn around your axis (figures 46a–c).

FIGURE 46 Try this drill where you totally focus on the correct body motion to feel a correct upper-body turn. (a) Start with your arms crossed over your chest. (b) Practice turning your shoulders; as you stay centered, your left shoulder should be behind the ball. (c) Next, practice turning through the ball so that your shoulders and hips are perpendicular to the target.

As I said in chapter 3, take care to keep your eyes level to the ground as you swing back. Your eyes actually have a huge influence on the shape of your swing. That makes sense when you think about it. If your head is tilted to one side or the other, your eyes will follow suit and you will swing either too flat or too steep (figure 47a).

In contrast, a level eye line will allow you to swing the club on plane and, as an added bonus, help you maintain your balance throughout the swing (figure 47b). It is, after all, a fact that our world is based on our relationship to the horizon. If you tilt the horizon line either up or down, your perspective changes with it. Try putting the clubhead down behind the ball with your head tilted to the right or left. Not easy, is it? Now imagine how hard it would be to hit the ball squarely with your head in that same position.

If you think that tilting your eyes may be causing you problems, wear a hat out on the range. You can use the brim to check that your eyes are both starting level and staying that way as you swing the club back.

a   b

FIGURE 47 (a) Tilting your head in the backswing will make it difficult to swing on plane. (b) Keeping your eyes level to the ground during the backswing is a key to having good balance.

One-Piece?

"One-piece" is a term that you hear a lot when the takeaway is being discussed. And it isn't necessarily wrong. For me, it is defined as the turn of your shoulders and the swing of your arms happening together. Together with your wrists hinging upward and your forearms rotating, it is really what your backswing is all about. Combined, those moves are what get the club moving on the correct plane (figures 48a and b).

Too much wrist cock, arm swing, or shoulder turn independent of one another is going to knock you off plane. If you have too much rotation in your hands and not enough wrist cock, the club will move too much to the inside or flat. If you cock your wrists without any rotation in your forearms, the club will be outside the correct line, or too steep. If you turn your shoulders without cocking your wrists, you will start the club back on too flat a plane. If you swing your arms back independent of your shoulder turn, your swing will either be too steep or too flat.

FIGURE 48 (a) Everything starts back together in a one-piece takeaway: the shoulders, arms, and hands all move together. (b) In a true one-piece takeaway, the wrists must start cocking right away in order to get the club up off the ground. You should never strive to keep the club low to the ground.

An on-plane swing, then, is always a combination of your wrists hinging, your arms swinging back and up, your shoulders turning, and your forearms rotating; most important is that they all move together and in sync with one another. Create the correct blend and your perfect swing is off to the perfect start.

Okay, now that we have an understanding of what you are trying to achieve, what does it look like?

The Backswing: In and Up

Because you are standing to the side of the ball, your club has to swing on an arc. So it has to move to the inside of a line drawn from the ball to the target. That's simple physics. The key then is finding that arc, the hard part of which is blending the "inside" part of your takeaway and backswing with the "up" part. It's a bit like rubbing your stomach and patting your head at the same time; it takes some practice to get it right.

There are two directions involved here: in and up. It's easy to go up without going in, and it's easy to go in without going up. The difficult part, as I said, is successfully blending the two so that the club swings on the correct plane. Every golfer is different in that respect. You will have a certain amount of "in" and a certain amount of "up" depending on your physical characteristics—your height, the length of your arms—and the distance you stand from the ball. What is certainly true, however, is that there will be a plane that is right for you no matter which point you are in your swing.

The "up" part of your backswing is a combination of a few factors. Again, because you are bent forward from your hips, the turn of your shoulders has some tilt to it, causing some "up." Your arms swing the club back and up. But the biggest factor in "up" is the hinging of your wrists, especially at the start of the swing.

Imagine you are standing at address. Now pick the clubhead straight up in front of your nose by hinging your wrists (figure 49). That is exactly the wrist motion you want to make in your backswing. Of course, it never looks like that in the golf swing because that motion is combined with your shoulder turn, your arm swing, and the rotation of your forearms.

In the early part of the backswing, you want to feel the sensation that the handle of the club is descending and the head of the club is coming up. You should feel as if you are pushing the club down with the back of your left hand and picking it up with your right forefinger, which acts as a sort of trigger on the grip (figure 50).

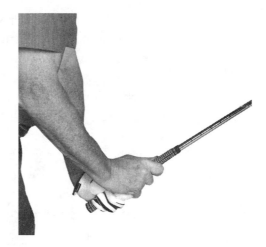

FIGURE 49 Correct wrist action in the golf swing would have your wrists cocking the club right up toward your chin.

FIGURE 50 In the takeaway, the butt end of the club should feel like it is going down as the clubhead is coming up.

At this point, don't worry about the phrase "picking the club up," one that is often used in a negative way in describing the golf swing. In fact, it really isn't something you can ever do too much. If you ever do fall into that trap and are taking the club too much outside, it will only be because you have not created the proper and balancing amount of rotation (figure 51). So the reality is that if you are picking the club up too much, it's not because you are picking the club up too much—stay with me now!—it is because you are not turning your shoulders and rotating your forearms at the same time. When that happens, you are simply out of sync or are disconnecting your arms from your body in the takeaway.

FIGURE 51 If your arms stay connected to your body and you turn your shoulders and rotate your arms, the club won't go outside, as shown here.

The opposite is also true, of course. If you move the club away from the ball too low and to the inside, it is because you have underdone the amount of wrist cock required to put you on plane. In other words, the problem is not that you are doing something too much, it's that you are not doing something enough (figures 52a and b).

a

b

FIGURE 52   (a) When the hands turn in the takeaway instead of the wrists cocking up, the club goes too much to the inside at the start of the swing. (b) The clubhead should be moving up and to the inside in the backswing in the takeaway.

When the Shaft Is Horizontal

For me, the takeaway ends when the shaft reaches horizontal to the ground and is parallel to the ball-target line (figure 53). At that point, your hands have moved to where they are just about over your right foot and the toe of the club has turned slightly, so that the angle of the clubface matches the angle of your spine. Take care, though. That doesn't mean that the toe of the club is pointing straight up, only that it is "toed in" a little.

FIGURE 53 This is a key checkpoint: in an on-plane takeaway, the club should be parallel to the ground and the target line at the same time.

I can't emphasize enough how important it is to make sure that when you swing the club back that the club passes through a point where the clubshaft is both parallel to the target line and parallel to the ground at the same time. Practice it again and again until you can do it without thinking. You need to do so because this is not a completely natural move. What happens is that the weighted part of the club is on the ground. Then it needs to come up. So you have to move something that is heavy off the ground. That isn't natural—or doesn't feel that way. In reality, it is more natural to keep that weight low to the ground, which is why you hear so much about "width" in your backswing.

Width

There are three components in every backswing plane: inward motion, upward motion, and backward (then forward) motion. The backward motion is really what constitutes the "width" of your backswing (figure 54).

There are two things that will create width: your shoulders turning, and the extension of your left arm as the club swings back (figure 55). The reality is that your arms stay in front of your body as it turns. When you set up to the ball, your arms are in front of you, and that is a relationship you want to maintain in the backswing.

FIGURE 54 Your arms should stay out in front of your shoulders as you turn in the backswing; this creates the width you need for a powerful and repeatable swing.

What commonly "narrows" a back-swing is the arms swinging in, too close to the body (figure 56). When that happens, your right arm gets too far behind you, and your left arm is too far across your chest. Alternatively, hanging on your left side—the so-called reverse pivot—into the backswing will have the same effect.

Think of width in these terms. It isn't something you are consciously trying to manufacture in your swing. Rather, it is

FIGURE 55 Practicing this move, where you turn and keep your arms out in front of you, without a club is a great way to get the feel for the correct turn and width in the backswing.

FIGURE 56 An incorrect position is where your right arm moves back too much and the left arm swings too much across your chest. The correct width in the backswing will be impossible to achieve.

something you have created at address and need simply to maintain as you swing back and through. With the exception of your shoulder turn, width is something you have before the club even begins to move. So there is no need to feel as if you have to "extend" anything. Don't ruin your swing by trying to make more of something you have plenty of already.

This exercise will give you the correct feeling. Without a club, stand as if at address, other than that your hands are not together as they would be on the club. Now, without turning, fold your right elbow up so that your arm forms a 90-degree angle (figure 57a). Then turn your shoulders, maintaining the relationship between your arm and your body (figure 57b). Now bring your left hand up to meet your right hand (figure 57c). That is the perfect backswing right there: your left arm straight but not stiff.

a   b   c

FIGURE 57 In order to get the feel for the correct width in the backswing, practice these moves. (a) First, bend your right elbow in front of your body. (b) Now, turn your shoulders, keeping your right arm in the exact same relationship with your body. (c) Finally, swing your left arm and hand up to meet your right hand, and you will have the feel for the correct backswing position.

From Parallel to the Top

From the end of your takeaway, the backswing is essentially a continuation of the moves you have already started. Your shoulders are going to keep turning and your forearms are going to keep rotating (figure 58).

In my experience, it is creating the correct amount of rotation in the forearms that causes a problem for most pupils. Here's how to feel the proper motion and the proper amount. Without a club, stand as if at address, your left arm hanging in front of you, the back of your left hand facing the target. Now turn your shoulders and using just one arm in the backswing, swing your left arm up

FIGURE 58 Your left arm gradually rotates in the backswing to keep the clubshaft on the correct plane.

to the top of the swing with just a gradual rotation as you go back and up. Your left wrist and left arm should be on a plane that is parallel to the original angle of the shaft at address, and you will be right on the correct plane (figures 59a and b). Then all you have to do to feel the correct plane in the throughswing is to do just the opposite with your right arm only. Turn your body through the shot and swing your right arm as you gradually rotate it through. The throughswing should be a mirror image of the backswing, and this drill will give you the feel of an on-plane backswing and throughswing.

a   b

FIGURE 59 (a) This drill, where you practice swinging back to the top of the swing with just your left arm, will teach you the correct swing plane and rotation in the backswing. (b) This drill, where you practice swinging through with just your right arm, will teach you the correct swing plane and rotation in the throughswing.

The next question, of course, is how quickly that arm rotation should occur during the backswing. Clearly you don't want all of it to happen at address or suddenly at the top of the swing. So the answer is "gradually." Every little bit of your backswing contains a corresponding amount of arm rotation. In other words, one-quarter of the way through your backswing, your arms should have rotated one-quarter of the correct amount. There is no point in your backswing where your arms are not rotating. Smoothness is important. The last thing you want in your swing is any sense of jerkiness (figures 60a–c).

That consistency of arm rotation is mirrored elsewhere in your backswing. As the club moves back, there is no point where it is not moving

FIGURE 60 (a) In an on-plane swing, the clubshaft is above but parallel to the original angle of the clubshaft at address. (b) The clubshaft maintains the same plane angle as the club moves up in the backswing. (c) Your left arm, left wrist, and clubface should all be on the same plane.

inward or upward. Everything is gradual and smooth, which is the real key to swinging on the correct plane. And by that I mean both the clubshaft and the clubface are on the plane.

More on the Plane

Your point of reference for what can, I know, be a difficult concept to grasp is the angle of the clubshaft. It should always be parallel to the angle you created at address (figures 61a–c). Note that I am not saying that it should always be *on* the original angle, only that it must be parallel to that line. As the club gets higher in the backswing, the shaft must move above its original angle, but it always should stay parallel to the original angle of the clubshaft at address.

a   b   c

FIGURE 61 (a) Here is the correct plane in the backswing, with the same clubshaft angle as at address. (b) Here the clubshaft is laid off the plane. (c) Here the clubshaft is at too upright a backswing plane.

FIGURE 62 Your left arm and left wrist should not form a straight line at address; when your arms are set right in front of your body at address, your left wrist will have just a little cup inward to it.

I recommend that you practice this part of the backswing in front of a mirror. You can even stick a piece of tape on the mirror so that it looks to you like it goes right over the original angle of the shaft at address as a reference point. What feels right in your swing isn't always necessarily so, and actually seeing what you are doing is an enormous help.

After a while, however, you will start to build a relationship between feeling and seeing. You will know what the correct plane feels like even without looking. Equally, you will know what it feels like when you are off plane. It helps to know both, though, especially as you are building awareness.

One reference point that will help you through this process is the little hinge in your left wrist at address. As you set up to the ball, your left arm and the club do not form a straight line; there is a little bit of an angle in your wrist (figure 62). That angle won't be there at impact. By then your weight will have shifted to your left side, your hands will be forward, and the back of your left wrist will be flat.

As you swing the club back and have the correct rotation of your arms, that angle in your wrist is disappearing. By the time you reach the top of the swing, your wrist should be relatively flat.

The End of the Backswing

You get to the end of your backswing when your shoulders have stopped turning. That's the easiest reference point. But everything in your backswing should be arriving at the same time (figure 63).

FIGURE 63 Your hands, arms, shoulders, and club should all reach the top of the swing at the same time.

When you see people making too long a backswing, their arms are swinging past their turn or they are letting go of the club at the top.

The length of your backswing is dictated by the turning of your shoulders behind the ball. There is nothing that says you have to swing to a definite point or distance. You don't have to swing the club to the point where the shaft is horizontal to the ground. But you don't have to stop it going there either. How long your backswing will be is dictated by your natural flexibility and your objectives.

If you are, for example, a short hitter, it may be that you should try to extend your backswing a little. And if you have distance to spare, a shorter backswing may give you a little more control. But whatever its length, your backswing must always be on the correct plane (figures 64a and b).

a   b

FIGURE 64 (a) A swing that is on plane and short of parallel should have the clubshaft pointing to the left of the target. (b) A swing that is on plane and reaches a point where it is parallel to the ground in the backswing should have the clubshaft parallel to the target line also.

You can be on the correct plane, of course, without getting anywhere near horizontal at the top of the swing. If you don't get there, the club will point to the left of the target at your "top." If you do get the club to horizontal, the shaft will be parallel to the target line. And if you go beyond that, it will point to the right of the target—"across the line," in golfing parlance.

How much any of those factors is present in your swing is

entirely dependent on the length of your backswing. Indeed, if you are like most people, you will be short of horizontal—and there is nothing wrong with that, as long as you are on plane. There is no rule that says you have to get the club all the way back to horizontal. Besides, the length of your arc is not how long your backswing is relative to horizontal; it is measured by the distance that the clubhead travels throughout the swing, so you can still have a big arc without getting all the way back to horizontal.

That's why those who tend to swing the club on too much of a straight line are going to have a tendency to overswing. They are not swinging on much of an arc, and the shortest distance between two points is a straight line, so they end up way past horizontal. On the other side of the coin, you can have a long arc without swinging the club anywhere near past horizontal at the top.

O'Meara's Backswing

It was October 1980 when I first started working with Mark O'Meara. At that time his backswing was real upright. He would drop the club to the inside on the way down and then flip his hands through impact. In other words, his downswing was compensating for the mistake he was making in the backswing. This was fine on days when his timing was good, but it wasn't so fine on days when it wasn't. We needed to "round off" his backswing and get it on a better plane.

So Mark and I started working together on that the first weekend we got together. We went onto the 14th hole on Pinehurst No. 4. In the process of working on his backswing, we got it flatter, but he still had a tendency to "stand up" on the way down. He was literally topping the ball.

The good thing was that he was willing to do what was necessary in order to make an effective change. Most people are not. With most students I am begging for an inch when I really want a foot. That wasn't the case with Mark. He changed a lot to begin with but didn't know how to react to those changes.

It must have been funny to watch and listen to. There I was telling him how much better his backswing looked. And there he was, a former U.S. Amateur champion and a tour player, hitting tops right along the ground. This went on for a while, until he turned to me and said, "Hank, that might be better, but I can't even make it to the ladies' tee!"

I told him not to worry and to stick with it. To his enormous credit, he did. And he got better. In fact, a couple of years later, Mark finished second on the PGA Tour's money list. Then, a year later, he found himself standing on the 18th tee at Pebble Beach with a chance to win the Bing Crosby Invitational. Like everyone who has ever played the game, doubt crept into Mark O'Meara's mind, and all he could seem to think about was how many times he had duck-hooked balls into the ocean playing that hole as a youngster. But he worked on getting his backswing more rounded and even went so far as to feel like he was so flat that he was going to swing right over the top of the ball. He kept telling himself that if he did that, at least he wouldn't go in the ocean.

Sure enough, he killed one right down the middle and went on to win. That was Mark's first of five wins at Pebble Beach (now the AT&T). It just goes to show you that it takes dedication and determination to change anything, and there is quite a difference between what something feels like and what it actually looks like. Don't be scared to exaggerate your changes. It will get you there a lot faster.

5 THE FORWARD SWING

The most important thing to realize about the backswing is that its biggest function is to set up the proper chain reaction for the downswing (figures 65a and b). One of the questions I am most often asked is, "How do I start the downswing?" To which I usually reply, "With your backswing!"

a

b

FIGURE 65 (a) Coiling correctly in the backswing is a key to starting down correctly. (b) Swinging the club up on the correct plane in the backswing gives you the best chance to start down correctly.

Let me explain. If you are worried about starting your downswing correctly, you are first making a lot of big assumptions. One, that your setup is correct. Two, that your takeaway is correct. Three, that your backswing is on plane. Four, that at the top of your swing you are not only in the right place but got there the right way. And five, that you are coiled correctly.

That's a lot to get right. But all those things have to happen before you have even a chance to start down correctly. It's this simple: if you don't wind up correctly on the backswing and swing the club on the correct plane all the way to the top, chances are you are not going to make a great downswing. All of which only underlines the importance of the previous chapter.

That's why I always put more emphasis on how the club gets to the top than I do on how it starts down. If you get the former right, chances that the latter will follow are increased greatly. Like I said, it's a chain reaction, although there are, of course, no guarantees.

Let's say that, for the last ten years, you have swung the club too much to the inside on the way back, then looped it "over the top" to the outside on the way down (figure 66). After

FIGURE 66 Coming over the top to start the downswing is the most common mistake amateur golfers make.

so long, you are used to that swing and it will be difficult to change. So you work at it and get your backswing on plane. That's great. But, sadly, fixing your backswing isn't necessarily going to fix every other fault in your total action. Chances are you will still have trouble with your downswing. It is another bad habit you have to break. So you work on that next.

Up and Down

Still photographs of golf swings in books and magazines are very useful tools in the teaching and learning of the game of golf. But make sure you take a little care when you are analyzing one part of the swing: the transition between the backswing and the downswing. I'm sure you have all seen great-looking pictures of amazing players at the top of their backswing. Fully coiled, the club perfectly horizontal, their eyes glued to the ball, those guys are surely in enviable positions.

There is, however, a catch. Because these pictures can never properly convey movement, they can be misleading. The fact is, there is a point at the top of the swing when a blend between the backswing and the downswing occurs. In other words, you are going in two directions at once.

The golf swing does not consist of backswing-stop-downswing. That is why you should never think of pausing at the top. Instead, realize that, as you change direction, not everything is doing so at the same time. The lower body, for example, is already heading back toward the ball and the target before the hands, arms, and club have completed their journey to the top.

This is especially noticeable in good players. As they swing back, they are already starting down. That is what creates the "lag" you want in the club at the start of the downswing. Lag is the storing of power, the holding of the angle in the club, the delay in uncocking your wrists—all before you release it through impact (figures 67a and b).

a   b

FIGURE 67 (a) Maintaining your wrist cock as you start down is a key to a powerful swing. (b) The longer and better you can maintain your wrist cock in the downswing, the better off you will be if you know how to release the club properly at the bottom of the swing.

The same phenomenon is obvious in other sports. If you watch a great angler casting, his rod is still going back as his hand comes forward. When a baseball pitcher throws, his arm is still going back as he takes his step forward prior to releasing the ball. In any sport where there is a back-then-forward motion, the forward part has started before the back part is completed.

That move is vital in creating that lag in the club and helps you with the timing of your swing. And the better you can do it, the more dynamic and powerful your swing and shots will become.

Starting Down

In chapter 4, I made much of the relationship between your hands and arms and your body. Well, the same is true of the downswing: you want your hands and arms to stay in front of your body.

Before that, however, we must deal with the often tricky subject of the transition between the backswing and the downswing. This, I know, is an area of great concern to many players, most of whom seem to have trouble smoothly blending the two together. Whether through anxiety and/or bad mechanics, so many golfers are too quick with the right side in transition.

What you need to do—as in every area of the swing—is to get your mind focused on what really matters, thereby excluding all the worries you may have about what might go wrong. So, as you get to the top of the swing then begin the downswing, feel as if your upper body stays where it is as your arms and the club begin their descent. Simultaneously, roll your right foot inward and make a slight lateral motion with your hips toward the target (figure 68).

That makes sense if you think about it, as you'd perhaps expect of a movement that is the opposite of the backswing. The backswing starts in your upper body, and the downswing starts in your lower body.

FIGURE 68 Your left hip should make a little bump forward in the downswing; this is what is called hitting into a firm left side. Practice this move by putting a club outside your left foot and moving forward into a solid left leg as you swing your right arm down.

In fact, your downswing starts from the ground up. At the top, with your weight focused on the inside of your right heel, your hips are turned maybe 45 degrees. So you are coiled like a spring, poised to move back in the opposite direction (figure 69).

That move starts in your feet. The first thing that happens is that you must push off the inside of your right foot, with your weight shifting all the way from the right heel to the left big toe (figure 70). That's the angle of your hips at the top of your swing, and that's the direction your lower body should initially move in the downswing. In conjunction, your hips start to rotate back toward their starting position at address.

As that is happening, your arms are dropping, lowering the club, with your left arm rotating back in to your side. Again, it is

FIGURE 69 If you turn your hips too much in the backswing, your lack of a proper coil will make it almost impossible to start the downswing correctly.

FIGURE 70 Shifting your weight in the direction of your hips from the top of the swing, the weight should move from your right heel to your left toe.

essentially the opposite move you made on the backswing, complete with the same rotation in your forearms, back to address.

All of that stems from the lead created by your lower body. Your feet, knees, and hips start to move, dragging the club with them. That, I'm sorry to say, is exactly the opposite of what I see in so many golfers who start the downswing with their upper bodies, usually their shoulders (figure 71a). Instead, get that feeling of your upper body staying at the top of your swing as your arms and club start to drop (figure 71b).

Within that broad description, there are some key points you should focus on from the top of your swing. The movement in your

FIGURE 71 (a) If you start the downswing with your shoulders, you will move out and in front of the ball. (b) Your back should feel as if it stays facing the target as you swing your hands and arms down to begin the downswing.

hips is not simply a turn back toward the ball. There has to be some lateral shifting that will transfer your weight back to your left side. If you fail to make this move, it almost ensures that you will come over the top, which is the most common mistake that amateurs make. When this happens, the club comes down too steep into the ball. Now, lateral shifting is not the same as "sliding" your weight toward the target. All that does is get your lower body too far ahead of the ball at impact, and in turn creates a swing that is likely to be coming into the ball too shallow and too much from inside.

Remember what I said about the shift of weight: it must follow the direction of your hip turn, on an angle from your right heel to your left big toe. In other words, your weight stays on the inside of your feet, not the outside, as you initiate the movement of your lower body at the start of the downswing.

Let your lower body take charge of leading the downswing; your upper body should be relatively passive in comparison. What you should be feeling is the rotation of your hips and the lowering of your arms and the club. This lowering movement combined with the rotation of your arms will allow you to swing the club on the correct plane. As you start down, the feeling will be that you are briefly re-creating that angle of your left wrist that you had at address, before you release into the ball and swing through. That first move down is something even the very best players rehearse a lot in slow motion (figures 72a and b). It helps them get the feeling of bringing the club down in front of them. Watch Tiger Woods; he works on that move a lot.

a

b

FIGURE 72 (a) The left wrist has flattened by the time the club gets to the top of the swing. (b) As the club starts down, the left wrist should feel as if it is cupping just a little in order to retrace the backswing coming down.

If you start your downswing with your upper body, the club will likely come down on too steep a plane (figure 73a). If your upper body races out ahead of your lower body, this can also cause your left arm to get pinned too much across your chest and the club will come down on too flat a plane and behind you (figure 73b).

FIGURE 73 (a) Starting down with your right shoulder out too much can cause the clubshaft to come down on too steep a plane. (b) Spinning the upper body out too fast to start the downswing can also cause the club to come down too flat and too far from inside and behind the body.

Checkpoints

In order to keep things as simple as possible, use the same checkpoints coming down that you used going back.

Halfway down you want the club to be back on plane (figure 74). When the club is parallel to the ground, it should also be parallel to the target line. Check the clubface at this point, too. If your right wrist is bent back too much, the clubface will be closed and

FIGURE 74 The clubface and the clubshaft should be on a plane that is parallel to but above the original angle of the clubshaft at address, as the arms bring the club down toward impact.

coming into the ball too much from the inside. If there isn't enough bend in the right wrist, the clubface will be open and heading into the ball from the outside.

It almost goes without saying, but do all of your checking in slow motion at this point. There is no way that you are going to be able to feel or see the proper moves if you are swinging at full speed or close to it. So do it all very slowly, in front of a mirror if you can.

In this instance, get into your top-of-the-backswing position, then feel—really feel—the rotation of your hips and the shift of weight onto your left foot.

Keep going all the way to impact, checking your swing plane all the way to the ball. When you come to strike the ball, your hips should have turned through more than your shoulders, just as in the backswing your shoulders turned more than your hips (figure 75). One key point as you rotate your body from the top of the swing down and to impact is that you maintain the same body angles throughout your swing; in other words, keep the posture you established at address.

Your left hand is a useful check-point, too. At the moment of impact, you want the back of your hand to be flat and looking directly at your target. Think of your hand as the clubface. Imagine you are slapping a wall with the back of your hand as the clubhead contacts

FIGURE 75 Your hips should be turned more than your shoulders at impact. Make sure you maintain your posture as you make the downswing and come into impact.

the ball. If you hit with either side of your hand, your clubface will be open or closed at impact, depending on which side of your hand slaps the wall (figures 76a and b).

Your knuckles are good guides here also. If they are looking skyward at impact you have, in effect, added loft to the shot. If they are looking toward the ground, the club delofted. The bottom line is that your arms continue to rotate through impact, with your wrists unhinging (figures 77a–e). The cocking of the wrists on the backswing has to be released as the club accelerates through the ball. Especially if you are prone to a slice, make this one of your key swing thoughts. Ben Hogan called this "supination" in his seminal book *Five Lessons: The Modern Fundamentals of Golf.*

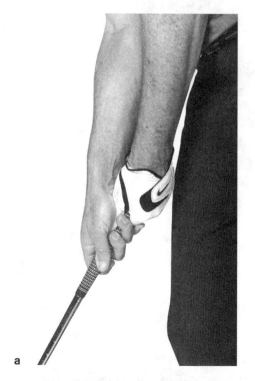
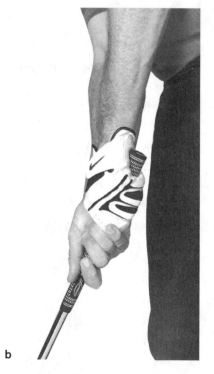

a   b

FIGURE 76 (a) If your hands turn over too much coming into the ball, the clubface will close too much and you will hit a hook. (b) If you "slap the wall" with the side of your left hand instead of the back, the clubface will be open and you will produce a slice.

FIGURE 77 (a) Your hands and hips lead the clubhead into impact. (b) Hitting into a firm left leg is a key to hitting solid shots with a square clubface. (c) A correct impact position is one in which the back of your left hand faces the target at impact. (d) Hitting on the collapse at impact leads to weak, high shots. (e) If your left wrist bows down too much coming into the ball, the shot trajectory will be too low.

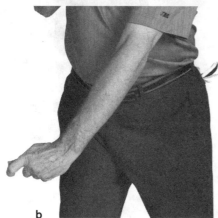

The Release

The release is the part of the golf swing that most players have trouble both understanding and achieving. Granted, a poor release of the club through impact can stem from many things: a poor setup, a faulty takeaway, an off-plane backswing, and a jerky transition, to name a few. But even if you do all or most of those things correctly, you still have to release the club properly.

When I am describing the release, I go back to the left hand. In any proper release of the club, the back of the hand—and so the clubface—is square at impact, there is the correct loft on the club, and the bottom of the swing is in the right place. Those are the three things you need to achieve if you are to hit a good shot (figures 78a–d).

You achieve all three of these objectives by correctly releasing your wrist cock. In the backswing, you hinge your wrists and rotate your body. In the downswing, you rerotate and hold that wrist hinge until you release it at the bottom.

FIGURE 78
Practicing the correct motion of the back of your left hand is the best way to get the feel of a correct release. (a) With just your left hand, start at address. (b) Hinge the left wrist as you swing back. (c) Square the back of your left hand as you release your wrist at impact. (d) Your left hand continues to supinate through the ball.

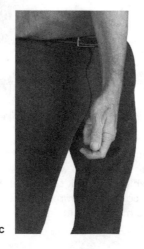
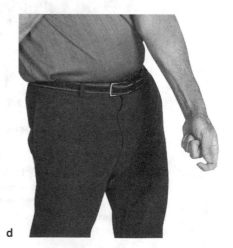

In sum, the release is a rerotation of your hands, arms, and body, combined with the unhinging of your wrists. In other words, it is the exact opposite of what you were feeling and creating in the backswing.

The feeling you should have in your hands is that the bottom of your right hand is pushing down as the bottom of your left hand pulls up. That gives you a proper release (figure 79).

Of course, all of this has to be timed properly, too. Your aim is to re-create at impact the shaft angle you had at address. If you release too early or too late, you will never achieve that. The full release, in fact, happens just after impact, the back of the left hand arched a little bit, just as if you are hammering a nail into a piece of wood. In golfing terms, that is the point of full extension—your arms straight and your wrists extended—which is where you want to reach on every normal shot (figures 80a and b and figures 81a–d).

FIGURE 79 The right wrist should be fully released just past the ball.

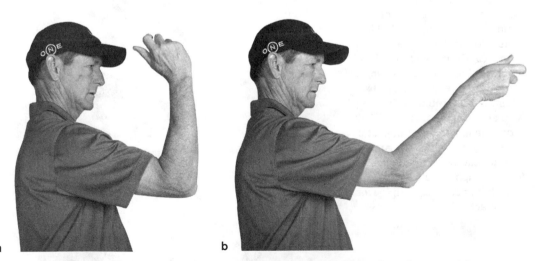

a   b

FIGURE 80 (a) To practice the correct release of the right hand, cock your wrist as if you were getting ready to hammer a nail. (b) Your right hand should be fully released through the ball in order to achieve the most solid and powerful hit.

FIGURE 81 (a) Maintaining your posture is important if you are going to reach the point of full extension with your hands and arms. (b) Coming into the ball, your right foot should roll in, but your right heel should still be close to the ground. This is key if you are going to attack the ball from the inside. (c) Just past impact, your hands and arms should extend to a full release. (d) The hips should open up as the club is coming from the inside to impact.

d

The Follow-Through

In many ways a good follow-through is the logical result of a good swing and release. If you have achieved the former, it is relatively easy to stay on plane to the end of the swing (figure 82).

But the follow-through is still worthy of study. Ideally, of course, it should be a mirror image of your backswing in terms of plane. A right-handed backswing is the same as a left-handed follow-through and vice versa. The only real difference is that there is more extension in the follow-through than on the backswing, no matter what side of the ball you stand on.

The checkpoints are the same, too. You want your club to pass through a point where the shaft is parallel to both the ground and the target line. Then, as you continue through, your hips and shoulders are rotating and so are your eyes. They should follow the club. You don't want your head and eyes rooted to the point where the ball was; that will tend to make your right hand "cross over" your left as you swing through. Instead, focus on rotating your body through the ball, your arms extending until your elbows start to relax, your belt buckle facing the target, and, finally, your wrists hinging (figures 83a–f).

FIGURE 82 A good follow-through is usually a result of a correct swing, but sometimes trying to finish in a correct position and on balance can have a positive effect on your whole swing.

FIGURE 83 (a) There should be a point of full extension where your arms, hands, and clubshaft are fully extended through the ball. (b) Letting your eyes follow the shot is a key to an unrestricted finish. (c) Your belt buckle should face the target at the finish of your swing. (d) The plane of your throughswing should be a mirror image of your backswing. (e) There should be barely any weight on your right foot at the finish of the swing. (f) Holding your finish for a second or two is a good habit that will teach you balance.

So don't neglect your follow-through. While it is obviously true that you can make improvements to your swing by working on it from beginning to end, the opposite is also true; you can make significant changes by working backward, from the end to the beginning.

If I'm trying to get somewhere, I can do it in a couple of ways. I can ask advice on a route—step-by-step directions—from someone who knows the way. I'll do that if I don't know the area at all. Or I can get there if someone tells where it is in relation to a place

I already know. The golf swing is the same way. You can go step-by-step from the beginning. Or you can work backward from a point you already know. When you think about how you want your swing to finish, that image will change the way you take the club back.

Take care, though. Make sure you use only the correct dosage when working end-to-beginning. For example, if you are working on, say, a feeling of swinging the club to the right through impact, it will only be a matter of time before you are taking the club back too much on the inside. That's only natural; such a move will make it easier for you to achieve your objective of swinging to the right through impact. So, without even thinking about your take-away, you have changed it by working on your throughswing!

Having said that, it is often the case that it is easier to feel something in your finish than in your downswing. The speed of the downswing is part of that. But when you concentrate on your finish and staying balanced, it helps you swing at a pace you can handle. If you weren't focused on your balance, the likelihood is that you would swing faster and faster until you fell over! So pausing your finish is one way to regulate the pace at which you are capable of swinging.

6 PRACTICE

The first thing that needs to be said about practice is that it is safe to assume that the vast majority of golfers don't do enough of it. Whether through lack of motivation, shortage of time, or lack of stamina, few of us get out on the range or practice green often enough. So it follows that we all need to make the most of whatever time we do have on what the old pros used to call "misery hill." That, sadly, isn't what I see too many people doing. For most of the people out there hitting balls, hitting balls is exactly what they are doing and only what they are doing; it certainly isn't real practice as I would define it. Indeed, it is nothing more than exercise (figure 84).

There's a big difference between real practice and just going through the motion of swinging and hitting balls out there somewhere. Those who are out there "exercising" try this, try that, and then they try this again. They go from one vague tip to

FIGURE 84 It isn't about how many balls you hit, it's about concentrating on each ball you hit.

105

another, all the time aimlessly hitting balls into the middle of a big field. Oftentimes they pay little or no attention to where the ball goes beyond grunting in frustration at yet another poor contact between club and ball.

Take it from me: that isn't practicing, it is searching—hoping to find something that works and then hoping it lasts.

Real practice is having a definite plan as to what you are working on. That can be written down or in your mind; it doesn't matter, as long as you have a plan. Before you even get out there you need to know what you are going to focus on, what elements of your swing you are going to try and improve. Then, when you do get onto the range, you stick to that plan, no matter how well or how badly things are going (figure 85).

If things aren't perhaps going as you would like, stop for a minute to reflect on exactly what you are doing. Analyze how you have been going about things. Make up your mind about what you need to do more, or less, or not at all. Is it time to move on to the next step? If you don't have that sort of agenda worked out beforehand, you aren't, as I said, really practicing. All you are doing is searching, usually fruitlessly, for something that might just work for a couple of days or rounds—if you're lucky.

None of it makes any sense. And you wouldn't do it that way in any other area of your life or in another sport. Let's say you are going to a practice session as part of a basketball team on a Tuesday evening. The coach, if he is any good, is going to have some drills for you to do with your teammates. Then you might scrimmage for a while. He will have a plan designed to make you better at certain aspects of the game you are playing. What he

FIGURE 85 Taking notes is a great way to make a plan and stick to it.

won't do is let you shoot lay-ups or free throws all evening while you chat with your friends.

So why is it that you go to the driving range and try every little tip you have ever heard or read? Why is it that you don't have a plan?

The first part of any plan is deciding just what it is you are going to work on. What fundamentals are you going to focus on? What clubs are you going to hit? How long are you going to hit for? How are you going to divide your time?

In answer to that last question, I recommend you spend about half of your practice time on the full swing and half on the short game. Half of your short game time should be spent on putting. And, yet again, make sure that you are actually practicing and not just wasting time. Think hard about what you are doing and make every shot count. Put some pressure on yourself to make the move you are trying to make or hit the shot you are trying to hit.

Know when to stop, too. If you are getting tired, call a halt. Once you are fatigued, you are probably not going to be as efficient as you need to be to successfully make changes to your game. Tiger Woods never practices for more than ten to fifteen minutes at a time without taking a little break. No one else I have taught does that. He might stop for only a minute or two, but he takes regular breaks. Here's the key, though. While he's standing there having a drink or whatever, he's thinking hard about what he just did or didn't do. He's thinking about his plan and about whether it needs some adjustment. He's thinking about what's next. Should he keep going with what he is working on, should he move on to the next point, or is it time to retrace his steps a little?

Of course, not all practice has to be done on the range. You can make swings in front of a mirror at home or with a video recorder if you have one. You can check your positions and perform little drills while swinging without a ball. For everything that happens before impact you don't need a ball, anyway. So you can work on your grip, your setup, your takeaway, your turn, your position at the top, and your swing plane without actually hitting a shot. There is so much you can do without leaving the house.

Practice Swings

As an extension of your work in front of a mirror or with the video recorder, when you do go out on the range, make practice swings a big part of your session. You can almost never make enough practice swings. I see so many people making thoughtless, nonchalant swings that do nothing but loosen them up a little. They are certainly no good in any practical sense. And they don't, to my mind at least, qualify as practice swings.

A real practice swing is one that simulates as exactly as possible the swing you want to make when you are actually hitting the ball. You can make that practice swing in slow motion, or half speed, or full speed, whatever gives you the best feel of what comes next. It doesn't matter.

That isn't the sort of practice swings I see too many club golfers making either on the range or on the course. In fact, many people don't take practice swings at all, not real ones. What they do is swish the club around, while they chat with their friends or think of nothing in particular.

That sort of inattention to detail is a huge mistake. Making practice swings—lots of them and real ones—is the best way I know for any golfer to improve. Pay attention to the professionals out on tour when you next see them on television. Almost every one of them makes a thoughtful practice swing before almost every shot. They do that for good reasons; they want to feel the swing they are going to make a few seconds later, and they want to get better.

That's why you should be working on your practice swing, too. Think about it. If you can make one, or two, or hopefully a series of perfect practice swings, eventually your mind and body are going to catch on and you will start making those great swings with a ball in the way. And when you start doing that, you are inevitably going to start hitting better shots and shooting lower scores.

It's just simple logic: if you can't make good practice swings, how can you possibly expect to make a good swing with the added pressure of having to hit a ball? Or if you can't make a good slow swing, how can you expect to make good fast swing? Or if you can't do it on the range, how can you expect to do it in a casual round? Or if you can't do it in a casual round, how can you expect to do it in a tournament? Or of you can't do it on the first hole of a tournament, how can you expect to do it on the last hole, when the pressure is at its greatest?

The answer to all of those questions is obvious: you can't.

The great thing about practice swings is that there are no rules attached to them. You can make them as fast or as slow as you like. You can make a half swing, a quarter swing, or a full swing. You can make part of a swing, starting from address, or the top, or even at impact. The choice is up to you: your practice swing is whatever you need to work on.

That's another thing about practice swings: they allow you to find a starting point for change. I tell all my students that if you are changing some aspect of your swing or your game, that change needs a starting point. Maybe you need to spend two weeks working solely on your takeaway before you can move on. Maybe you spend those two weeks making slow-motion takeaways. It doesn't matter, as long as you know where to start, where you are headed, and how many steps are involved in getting you there. Which brings us back to having a plan.

Stick with It

There is always a temptation whenever you see some improvement in your shots or your swing to skip a step or steps in your plan. Don't do it. If your plan is a good one, one that is going to effect lasting change for the better, work through every step. Don't imagine that you can get to where you want to go quicker than you first imagined.

So, if you are, say, only halfway through your prescribed plan and you have already had some success and hit some good shots, never think that you have reached the promised land early. The likelihood is that if you haven't finished the course of medicine, the disease or virus is going to return, sooner rather than later. Never release yourself from the "hospital" early.

Besides, golf being the game that it is, thinking you have got or found "it" is, while something to be enjoyed, only temporary. No one ever gets "it" for very long. But here's the thing. If you have followed your plan to the end and played well, regaining your form is going to be easier than it was the last time you were playing poorly. In other words, your next plan will be shorter.

Retrace Your Steps

Actually, the likelihood is that if you have done really well at something, you don't need a new plan at all. This is something I tell all of my students. If you know how to get someplace and you lose your way, all you have to be able to do is retrace your steps. If you are like every golfer I have ever met, your swing will have certain tendencies and you will have poor shots that you will fight your whole golfing career. That's true of everybody. It's a fact of golfing life.

Don't think of retracing your steps as going backward. Going backward is not retracing your steps. Let's say you took five steps to get to where you wanted to be. You worked hard on all five, in sequence, and now you're hitting the ball great. It is at this point that human nature kicks in. That little voice in your subconscious tells you that the reason you are playing so well is that last thing you did, step five in the sequence.

Anyway, you are out there focusing on good old number five. Things are still going well. Then you start to hit the odd loose shot. Then you hit a few more. Suddenly, you're not hitting it as well as you were. So what do you do? You try number five again. No change. So you try it some more. Now you're almost as bad as you were before you got to number one and panic is setting in.

What you should have done, of course, is go back to number four as soon as it became clear that number five wasn't working.

Then number three, number two, and number one. You should have retraced your steps until you started to see some improvement.

That makes sense when you think about it. If you know how to get to a place—and you have been there before—by turning three corners, all you have to do is retrace your previous journey. You could try a shortcut, of course. But if you do, you risk getting lost. The same is true in the golf swing.

True confidence is knowing that if you retrace your steps, you will get there. The trouble is, not everyone has the patience for that. Everyone wants to be hitting the ball great when they leave the practice tee so that they can sleep soundly. But that is invariably a transient feeling. Real confidence is being able to know, even halfway through the process, that retracing your steps is the best way to get to where you want to go, even if, when you leave that range, you haven't quite gotten there yet.

Make that your practice mantra. Retrace your steps all the way back to step one if you have to, rather than hammering away at step five. In the end, that is always a losing battle.

Know Your Distances

One of the most important aspects of good ball striking is being able to control the distances that you hit your irons. You learn this in practice by always paying attention to how far you are hitting each shot; it is a vital part of proper practice. Professionals do this after every shot. They want to know what every shot felt like relative to the distance that it flew. In particular, they want to know what a shot that flew, say, ten yards too far felt like. Then they store that information. The more information you have in your brain, the more information you are going to have to draw on when it is time to make a decision on the golf course. You must know—or find out—how far you hit each club, under all kinds of situations.

There are a few things that influence how far you hit the ball with each club. The kind of ball you are using is one factor. The wind and the temperature are others. Be aware that you lose two yards for every ten degrees the temperature drops. That's why your shots don't fly as far in cold weather. Altitude also comes into play.

Whatever conditions or locations you are playing in, however, you need a starting point for your calculation of first how far a particular shot is playing, then what club you are going to hit. Make it easy on yourself, too. Almost every club has 150-yard markers on every hole. So start by figuring out what club you ordinarily need for that distance.

Next, figure out how big of a gap you have between clubs. As a general rule, it is usually about eight to ten yards between each one.

When you have all of the above information—you only need one good shot with each to find out how far you hit every club in the bag—you are ready to play. You are also equipped, it must be said, to eliminate what is surely the curse of many amateur golfers—coming up short because they overestimate how far they can hit each club.

What You Need to Work On

Here's another thing about "practicing" that isn't really practice. Don't go out on the range with your favorite club or clubs. Presumably, you are already confident with them and hit them well. So what is the point in practicing with them?

Instead, work on the clubs you are struggling with. The best way to build a repeating a swing and then maintain it is through playing a variety of shots. What that means is developing an ability to curve the ball from left to right and from right to left and being able to hit the ball high or low. If you can do all of those things, your practice time should be devoted to the shot that is most difficult for you to play.

No matter how accomplished you become at this infuriating

game, you are always going to have strengths and, at best, relative weaknesses. There are always going to be shots you are going to find more difficult to hit than others.

In other words, if you find that you are hitting the ball higher than you would like or higher than you do normally, go to the range and practice hitting low shots. If you are hitting lower than you want, get out there and work on high shots. If you are good at fading the ball but struggling to hit a draw, then you know that your swing is biased in that direction. So practice the opposite ball flight. The great Sam Snead used to do that after a round he was less than happy with. If he had been hooking the ball too much, he would spend an hour after signing his card hitting slices. That's the best way I know to get your swing back on track.

Indeed, even if you are not struggling with any aspect of your swing to any great extent, it is never a bad idea to keep it in balance by hitting a variety of shots. And you do that by hitting draws, fades, high shots, and low shots. If you ever get the chance to see Tiger Woods on the range at a PGA Tour event, watch what he does.

When he's warming up, Tiger might start with a few practice swings where his follow-through is more curtailed than normal. That means he's going to hit a few low shots. Then he'll make a very different-looking swing with a longer follow-through. That means he's about to hit some high ones. Then he'll move on to fades and draws, all preceded by the appropriate practice swings.

Once you know what Tiger is doing, you should be able to predict pretty accurately what shot follows what practice swing. Only rarely will he hit the same shot more than a couple of times in a row. And he will never hit a shot without first picking out the trajectory and distance he wants. But all the time he will be hitting that wide variety of shots—all to keep his swing in balance. He is, without question, the greatest most thoughtful practicer whom I have ever seen in the game.

Which is not to say that Tiger hits the ball as well as he would like every time he plays or practices. Like you and me, he is human. So, relative to his talent level, he struggles sometimes, too. On any given day, he pays attention to his tendencies, especially if he is headed out to play rather than just beat balls. By doing that, he knows what shots he might want to stay away from that day, what shots he should gravitate toward, particularly under pressure, and, generally, where his swing is. If he is having trouble hitting, say, a high fade, that tells him that his setup or swing needs some adjustment.

Those are the sorts of things that make Tiger's practice sessions unique in my experience. He does a lot of it in his mind, visualizing what he is trying to do and not do. He often uses a weighted club, where he works on the feel of whatever aspect of the swing he is concerned with. He takes a lot of slow practice swings. He even hits balls with that slow swing, hitting the ball maybe 50 yards.

Tiger always has a plan when he goes to the practice tee. He makes an enormous number of practice swings. And he varies his shots to keep his swing in check. So should you.

Warming Up versus Practice

Any part of any golfing day starts with a little warm-up. Do a little stretching. Hit some short irons, just to loosen up. Just about every pro on tour starts off that way. Work your way through the bag to the driver, then work your way back again. You're ready to go.

A full-blown practice session is similar in that you should work your way through the set. Start with short shots and progress to the longer ones. As for a plan within that rough guide, let me start by saying there aren't enough hours in the day to practice golf. But the more time you can put in, the more you are likely to benefit. In that respect, golf is like anything else in life.

Having said that, at this point in many instruction books the author would be giving you a minute-by-minute run-through of just what you should be doing if you have, say, an hour on the range. I'm not going to do that. The aim of this book and this chapter is not to dictate to you what to do. I want you to figure it out for yourself, based on the big picture I have described.

Besides, how can I possibly devise a program for you without actually seeing your swing and its various tendencies? The answer is I can't. No book can. If you are like most every other golfer on the planet, your practice is going to be a lot like putting out fires. You'll be working on the part of the game where you are struggling at that particular time.

But, as I hope I have done here, what I can help you with is to come up with your own plan and show you how to use it to its best effect. In other words, my aim is not to teach all of this to you. Instead, I am here to help you learn it. That is a very different thing.

Tiger's Warm-up

I make it a point to notice everything that Tiger does a little differently from the other some two hundred touring pros whom I have taught in my career. One of those things is the way he warms up before a tournament round. The first thing Tiger does every tournament day before he goes to the practice tee is have Steve Williams, his caddy, get him the pin sheet for the day. The pin sheets on the PGA Tour tell the players exactly where each pin is on the greens. Tiger studies that pin sheet like someone studying for a test. He wants to see where all the pin placements are, whether he will have to hit a draw to the pin on hole 3 or a fade to the pin on hole 6, whether he will have to hit a low shot into hole 9 or a high shot into hole 12. The whole time he asks Steve where all the tees are for the day, whether they are up on some holes or back on other holes compared to the day before, so that he can get an idea of what clubs he will be using on certain shots. Then taking the day's wind into consideration, he hits the shots that he will most likely hit with the clubs that he will most likely be using on key holes. During Tiger's warm-up, he practices all the shots that he feels will be critical to his round that day. Every five minutes or so he will pull that pin sheet and his yardage book out of his pocket and he will be thinking about what shot he will need on a certain hole. So it isn't just a case of loosening up; he is really preparing for his round. At the same time, Tiger is working on his swing and figuring out exactly what swing thoughts he is going to go with that day starting out in his round. I have never seen another touring professional warm up with so much focus on the course in addition to his swing.

Tiger's Practice

As you can tell, Tiger practices like no other player I have ever seen. He concentrates every minute he is out there, thinking carefully about what he is doing. And he makes every shot count. He doesn't hit a lot of balls in succession without pausing to reflect on what he has just done. From what I have heard, Jack Nicklaus practiced much the same way.

Tiger makes a lot of practice swings. He works in front of a mirror. He makes many swings with a weighted club. When he hits balls, he shapes the shots: left to right, right to left, and high and low. He never hits more than a few of each before switching to another. He's always trying to find the middle ground with his swing, and he does that by playing shots of all shapes and trajectories.

What really sets Tiger apart, at least in terms of practice, is how he prepares for tournaments. When he comes back from long layoffs, he invariably plays well. He has a great record in events right after he has been absent from the tour for a while. That's not a coincidence.

Practicing for the majors is another level. You can't just turn up at the Masters, U.S. Open, British Open, or any other stop on the PGA Tour and hope that you will play well. And the only way you can know where you stand when you arrive—what shots you have and don't have—is by preparing for those weeks in a way that will see you peak when you get show up at the tournament.

Tiger has a pretournament routine that is pretty intensive. I always go to Orlando to work with him in the weeks before the majors. Every day is about getting ready for the upcoming major.

His day typically starts at about 6:00 a.m.

He'll do some cardio exercise; maybe run four or five miles.

He'll spend an hour and a half in the weight room until 8:30 a.m.

Then he eats breakfast.

From 9:00 to 10:30 a.m. we are on the range.

From 10:30 to 11:30 a.m. we are on the practice green.

Then we will play nine holes.

Then we have lunch.

We are back on the practice tee for an hour and a half from 1:00 to 2:30 p.m.

From 2:30 to 4 p.m. we are on the pitching and chipping greens.

Then we play nine more holes.

We are back on the practice tee for half an hour from 5:00 to 5:30 p.m., working specifically on the thoughts he has gathered that day. He'll hit shots he has worked on, usually those he knows he will need during the tournament.

Then we are back on the putting green and he putts from 5:30 to 6 p.m.

That's at least a twelve-hour day. And in the evening, while he's watching television, he is invariably up swinging a weighted club during the commercials. He does that every day. His work ethic and dedication are second to none. I know other players on tour work hard, too. Vijay Singh is legendary for his practice routines. Padraig Harrington is another one who comes to mind when I think about players with a great work ethic. But if anyone works harder than Tiger Woods, they must somehow have more than twenty-four hours in their day. It's not just the time that he puts in on the practice tee—he is always thinking about what he needs to do to get better. He is simply amazing. If you want to get better at golf, you don't need to blaze a trail to find the way because Tiger Woods has shown you the road map. Hard work is what it takes.

7 ON THE COURSE

As you will have gathered from the previous chapter on practice, I am a big fan of organization when it comes to golf. I like to feel as if everything I am doing has a reason behind it and a purpose. Anything else is just a waste of time.

This is true on the golf course as well as on the range.

Pre-Shot Routine, Tactics, and Strategy

Even before you have decided what club you are going to use and what shot you are going to hit, you must know where you want to hit the ball—and, just as importantly, where you don't want to hit the ball. If you are going to miss your target, there are bad spots to miss and good spots to miss. So you better know where the good spots are.

The good news is that most golf shots don't call for you to hit the ball into an exact spot. But you are required to hit into a certain area. And some of those are better than others. So you need to figure out where you want to go and, in turn, where you don't want to go.

FIGURE 86
A correct pre-shot routine always starts with you behind the ball looking at the target and visualizing your shot.

Based on that information, your next step is to figure out what sort of shot you are going to play. Do you want to curve the ball from left to right or right to left, or hit a straight one? Do you want to hit it high or punch it low, or hit the shot on your normal trajectory?

Based on that decision, you can then pick out the club you are going to use. The factors involved in choosing a club are the lie of the ball, how far it is to the target, where is the pin placement, the direction of the wind, and the topography of the course (is the shot uphill or downhill?). All the while, you are taking account of where you very definitely don't want to go.

While you need to be aware of the possible bad consequences of hitting any shot, there is no need to spend too much time overemphasizing any negatives. Having said that, of course, knowing and recognizing the inherent danger of a shot is simply playing the game. We're all human, so a big part of golf is hitting better bad shots than anyone else. And a key to hitting better bad shots is knowing where not to miss.

Besides, it just isn't possible to play a course and not be aware of the trouble on the left or the right, or short or long. You have to take those issues into account. You have to know which side is worse than the other. That's just being realistic. I mean, if you are teeing off on a hole where there is water up the right side and no trouble to the left, it makes sense to err a little left of center. That's how even truly great players play the game. They don't stand up on the tee and fear the water. Instead, they focus on where they want to hit the ball. But where they want to hit the ball takes into account where they don't want to hit it. That's the real key.

So the first part of your pre-shot routine is visualizing the shot you want to play and picking the club best suited to achieving that aim. Only then should you go into the physical part of your routine. Every golfer I know, especially the ones who play the game well, has a little routine they go through before every shot. They all start from behind the ball, where they visualize what shot they want to play (figure 86).

That can sometimes be a little more complicated than it first sounds. If you have more than one option as far as the shape and the trajectory of the shot are concerned, play the shot you know is easier for you. Draw on your past experience. You will know what shape of shot you prefer to hit.

For example, if the pin is cut way to the left side of the green, the ideal shot is one that starts in the center of the putting surface and draws to the hole. Equally, if the pin is located well to the right, a ball fading off the middle of the green will have more chance of finishing close. But the likelihood is that one or another of those shots is going to be more difficult for you to play with the level of accuracy needed. When that is the case and you are faced with your least favorite option, play for the middle of the green, two putts, and a safe par. Aim for where a straight shot won't hurt you. In other words, know when to pick your battles.

Be aware that knowledge of yourself, your game, and your swing is a day-to-day thing. That safe little fade you rely on nine days out of ten isn't always going to be there. On that one other day you are going to have to come up with an alternative play— even the very best players have to do that on occasion. The key is recognizing when and where you just don't have that shot. So never be afraid of taking the more conservative route and taking any potential trouble out of play. There's nothing wrong with that.

Okay, we're still behind the ball, looking at the target. Now move forward into your address position. As you do so, pick out an intermediate target a few feet to a few yards in front of the ball and directly in line with the spot on the fairway or green you are aiming for. Jack Nicklaus famously did this—Tiger Woods does it, too—recognizing that it is much easier to line up on a target two yards away than one two hundred yards distant. It just makes too much sense not to do it.

Line your clubface up with the intermediate target first. Then take your stance, right foot first, make the final adjustments to your grip, then your left foot, so that the line across your toes is parallel to the ball-target line, forming the "railroad track" we discussed in chapter 3 (figures 87a–c).

FIGURE 87 (a) Always step into the ball with your right foot first and set your club down behind the ball with the clubface square to your intermediate target. (b) Then check to make sure the clubface is square. (c) Next place your left foot so that your stance is parallel to the left of your target for a normal shot. (d) Looking back down at the ball, make sure you are lined up to your intermediate target.

Now check that your knees, hips, shoulders, and eyes are also parallel to the ball-target line, assuming you are playing a standard, everyday shot (figure 87d). And, yes, this is basic stuff. But if you don't get your setup right every time, even a golfer with the best swing in the world is going to have a hard time hitting balls where they are supposed to go. So this is worth a few seconds of your time before every shot.

Over the Ball: The Waggle

The waggle is a much overlooked and much neglected part of the golf swing, which is too bad. A good waggle can do a lot of good for your swing. It loosens you up, alleviates tension, and gives you a preview of your swing's direction and pace. In essence, you are practicing the part of the takeaway most people get wrong (figure 88).

FIGURE 88 When you waggle, be relaxed and just move the club with your hands. There should be no shoulder turn or arm swing.

I see this all the time. An awful lot of golfers have trouble with just how their hands take the club away from the ball. They don't hinge their wrists up correctly. Instead, they tend to roll their hands rather than cocking their wrists up. All of this makes a good waggle even more important: the first move into the backswing is something a huge number of golfers need to practice (figures 89a and b).

a   b

FIGURE 89 (a) Waggle the club correctly, with your hands bringing up the clubhead. (b) If you waggle the club too much to the inside, you will take it too low and to the inside every time. Most people rehearse exactly what they do wrong in their takeaways.

The waggle is also important in that it is a move that is part of every shot in golf: even pitching, chipping, and hitting sand shots. Any kind of short shot uses a swing that is basically an extension of the waggle. Indeed, the same can be said for the full swing. All that changes is the length of the extension. So if you can make a good waggle, it is going to make a huge difference in your ability to make a correct swing on a consistent basis. It is simply a way for you to practice your swing. So spend a lot of time getting it right.

Sometimes your waggle needs to be slow and deliberate. Other times it needs to be quicker. But at all times it is a preview of the shot you are about to play. For example, if you are going to hit a high, soft lob shot over a bunker, you need to make that long, slow waggle, because that is the type of shot you are trying to produce.

Then again, you might be attempting to hit a real "spinny" shot out of a greenside bunker. So this time your waggle will be shorter and quicker, because that shot requires that type of swing.

As far as the full swing is concerned, use your waggle to preset the rhythm of the swing you want to make and also its direction. Those are the most important aspects.

I see so many people waggling the club without realizing that they are actually doing it. Every time you move the club you should be, in a sense, practicing some aspect of your swing. But aimless swishes or, even worse, a waggle that previews a poor takeaway or backswing are only going to hurt you.

The most common mistake I see is where a golfer waggles the club so that it goes back to the inside and "underneath" his arms. That's natural, at least in that everything at address is geared to pull you to the inside. You are standing to the side of the ball. Your hands are above the clubhead. The clubhead is like a heavy weight at the end of a stick and you must hinge your wrists up or the clubhead will go back too low. To get the clubhead to come up, you have to hinge your hands and wrists. And you really don't have to try to take the clubhead to the inside, all you have to do is turn your shoulders and the clubhead will naturally come to the inside as long as your arms stay connected to your body.

That sort of lazy waggle is the start of something wrong. Be disciplined. Know that a waggle is not a movement of your body or your arms. Move the club only with your hands and wrists, so that it becomes a combination of wrist hinging and a little hand rotation (your right elbow bending just a little bit also). The former gets the club moving up a little; the latter provides a little inside motion. Thus it is a mini-swing or mini-takeaway, a preview of what is to come.

Don't go too far, though. The club should move only about halfway to your first swing checkpoint, where it is parallel to the ground. Any farther than that and your waggle becomes a full-blown takeaway or even a practice swing.

As you are waggling, take an occasional glance at the target. How many times you waggle is really up to you. But take some "advice." Find a good player you enjoy watching. Take note of his waggle and pre-shot routine. Then model yours on his and do the same routine every time.

To be honest, I'll be surprised if you can find too many differences beyond mannerisms in most pre-shot routines. Every player approaches the ball from behind. Every player visualizes the shot, then steps into the address position. But the number of times you waggle and look at the hole is worth copying. Two or three times will be enough of each.

One more thing: as they waggle, most players are moving their feet. Not a lot, but their weight is moving just enough that they don't get too static at the beginning of the swing. Starting from a dead standstill position is surprisingly hard to do and not advised.

8 WORKING THE BALL AND SHAPING SHOTS

The two components for this chapter actually have to do with marrying your shots to the conditions and contours of the land. When you have total control of your ball flight, there are nine types of shots that you can hit. There are three flights a ball can take in terms of curvature: straight shots, left-to-right shots, and right-to-left shots. And there are three different trajectories that each shot can take: low, normal, and high.

Now, that sounds like a lot to learn, and it is. But if you are like every other golfer I have ever met or watched on the range, at least one of the nine shots, maybe two, is going to come quite easily for you. We all have certain tendencies and preferences in life, and nowhere is that more true than on the golf course.

On the other side of that coin, of course, is that at least some of the shot shapes or trajectories are going to require you to get out of your golfing comfort zone. If your stock shot is, say, a little fade with a low trajectory, hitting a high controlled draw isn't going to be the most natural thing in the world for you.

Still, any and all of the work required of you in this chapter is going to be well worth the effort. Not only will you have a better understanding of what it takes to curve the ball in the air and control your shots' trajectory, but your overall swing will benefit from the balancing it will undergo as you work toward learning how to hit all nine shot shapes with equal ease.

In a perfect world, you would be able to hit straight shots, draws, and fades, normal-trajectory shots, high shots, and low shots at will. In other words, your fades wouldn't necessarily be high and your draws low. You'd be out there smacking high draws and low fades to order. But if you could do all that, your swing would indeed be perfectly in balance, perfectly neutral. You'd have all nine shots.

That is utopia, of course. But it is also true that you don't need all the shots to play very good golf. There have been plenty of examples of players who have won many championships and tournaments while hitting the same shape of shot almost every time. I'm thinking of men like four-time British Open champion Bobby Locke, who aimed way right and hit a massive draw. Lee Trevino won six majors on the back of his beautifully controlled left-to-right shot. So it can be done—and very successfully.

The best ball strikers—and the golfers I have just mentioned are among the very best of any era—controlled their distance through their trajectory. So should you. Standing over a shot of, say, 150 yards with an 8-iron in your hands, you have to hit the ball that distance by finding the right trajectory. That will vary from day to day, of course. There is always wind to take into account, as well as whether the shot is uphill or downhill.

Yet again, this is all about simple logic. A well-struck high shot is obviously going to carry farther than an equivalently struck low shot. So one way you can take a few yards off a shot is by flighting it a little lower. Likewise, if you are trying to get every yard you can from a club and a shot, you are going to need your optimum trajectory to achieve that.

So, rather than varying your distance with only the length and speed of your swing, get that same control with the trajectory of the shot.

Having said that, the more confident you are over as many different kinds of shot as possible, the better your chances of both playing and scoring well. The bigger your comfort zone, the better off you will be.

It is also important to realize that your comfort zone is going to vary in size almost every day. What was straightforward for you on Monday may not be so simple on Wednesday. But in the bigger picture, it is almost certainly true that the shots you are most comfortable playing will not alter much over time.

The ultimate ball striker, however, is one who cannot only hit the ball a long way, but who can hit all the shots, on many different trajectories. He can draw approach shots into back-left pins. He can feather a fade into a front-right hole location. He can hit the low run-up. He can smash a high one. And he can do all of this while controlling his trajectory. You can never be considered a great ball striker if you can't control your trajectory. Think back to the 2006 British Open at Hoylake. Tiger Woods won that event with a display of ball striking and control of trajectory that has only rarely been matched. Even for a man as talented as Tiger, that week stands out in memory.

Right to Left/Left to Right

If you are comfortable playing a slight draw or fade, all you are trying to do is change the arc of your swing a little bit. In general, the more you swing the club to the left and on a little less of an arc, the more you are going to tend to fade the ball (figure 90a). In achieving that, you need more emphasis on your body turn on the forward swing, a move that slows down the natural closing of the clubface through impact.

The opposite is also true. When you swing the club more to the right and on more of an arc, the clubface will close more than normal through impact, producing a draw (figure 90b). The more you slow down the turn of the body and increase the speed up the hands and arms, the more you will draw the ball. The more you speed up the body and slow down the club, the more you are going to hit fades.

a   b

FIGURE 90 (a) Intentionally pointing the club to the left at the top of the swing will promote a fade or slice. (b) The more the club points to the right at the top of the swing, the more it will swing into the ball on an arc from the inside, which will promote a draw or hook.

The Fade

When you want to play a fade, you need to adjust your ball position by moving it forward one or two ball widths, toward the target, and you need to adjust your alignment so that you are aimed about five to seven yards to the left. Obviously, the bigger the fade you are trying to play, the more forward your ball position will be and the more left you will want to aim. All of this will incline your swing plane to the left of the target, delay the closing of the clubface, and allow your body to clear through impact faster. Each of these things encourages a left-to-right shape of shot (figure 91).

FIGURE 91 Open your setup to the left a little to promote a left-to-right shot.

As you'd expect, hitting a fade will feel a little bit different from your stock straight shot. When you hit that straight shot, you swing the club on an arc that goes from inside to straight and to inside. That arc is different when you hit a fade. Instead of the face-closing effect caused by swinging on your natural arc, there is going to be a face-opening effect (figure 92a).

One place where that is especially noticeable—other than at address—is at the finish of your swing. If you have hit your fade, the reversal of the arc will produce a more upright finish than normal (figure 92b).

a   b

FIGURE 92 (a) Reversing the arc of your throughswing from impact to the finish will cause a left-to-right ball flight. (b) The more you finish with the clubshaft pointing up, the more your clubface will have had a tendency to stay open at impact, which causes a fade.

The Draw

This time your adjustments are made in the opposite direction. Move the ball back in your stance a little—about one or two ball widths is perfect—and align yourself about five to seven yards to the right of the target. The more you are trying to draw the ball, the more you will aim to the right and the more you will move the ball back in your stance. That will incline your swing plane in that direction, increase the speed at which the clubface closes through impact—slow your body turn this time—and place more emphasis on your hand action, all of which encourage the ball to curve from right to left (figure 93).

FIGURE 93 Align the clubface and your body to the right to promote a right-to-left shot.

Again, there will be a different feel hitting this shot. The arc this time will be more to the inside than it was for your straight shot, thereby closing the face quicker (figure 94a). And this time you will finish with the club more around your body (figure 94b).

a   b

FIGURE 94 (a) The more the club swings on an arc through the ball, the more the clubface will close, creating a draw shot. (b) Finish with the clubshaft pointing down your back more if you want to get the clubface to close, creating a draw shot.

Higher and Lower

A couple of things will produce an abnormally low shot: a lack of loft on the club at impact, or a lack of clubhead speed. The more speed you have, the more spin you arc going to put on the ball and the higher it is going to fly. That's why powerful players get such great hang time on their shots, and why the best long-iron players throughout history have all been strong and fast; they can get balls up in the air easier than someone who can't create the same amount of clubhead speed.

In contrast, a player who can't get as much clubhead speed is naturally going to hit the ball lower. His slower swing speed creates less spin and makes it harder for him to get the ball airborne. The other way to hit low shots, of course, is by delofting the club through impact.

The Low Shot

Okay, I'm faced with a situation where I need to hit the ball lower than normal, under some branches maybe. Or maybe I am hitting into the wind and the pin is located toward the rear of the putting surface. In either case, I want the ball to come out low.

The first thing I'm going to try to do here is slow down my swing. That's why you always hear people saying they took more club and gripped down when hitting into the wind. Gripping down the handle makes your arc shorter, and taking more club than you would normally need means you can make less of a swing and still hit the ball the required distance. Less of a swing means a slower swing.

The other influence on the height of the shot is the way you release the club through impact. For a low shot, you want to make an abbreviated finish, focusing on the extension you get out of your hands (figure 95a). It should feel as if your hands, arms, and the club are forming a straight line and your elbows are relaxing to break the momentum in the club (figure 95b). Try this a few times,

a

b

FIGURE 95 (a) The more you shorten your finish and extend the club and your arms to a straight line, the lower the shot you will hit. (b) For a low shot, break the momentum of your swing by softening your elbows while maintaining the extension in your hands and wrists.

making sure the clubhead never gets above your hands in the follow-through, and then grow your swing from there. This is the shot that everyone calls Tiger's stinger. I remember the first time I tried to explain how I believed this was the best way to hit this shot to Tiger. He didn't think he could do it, but years later it is one of his best shots.

In 1998, I went to the Dunhill Cup at St. Andrews with my student Mark O'Meara. He had won the Masters and the British Open that year, so he made the U.S. team along with Tiger and John Daly.

It was a very windy week and the course played hard. One day we were on the range and Tiger appeared (this, of course, was long before we started working together). Mark and I were working on hitting low shots into the wind, especially one that he would need at the short 11th hole. As we did so, Tiger mentioned that he didn't really have that shot. The only low one he had was the result of putting the ball back in his stance and "leaning" on the ball through impact. That produced a left-to-right flight that was less than ideal when the wind was into him and off the left.

The ideal shot, of course, was a low draw that would hold the ball up into the wind. But that wasn't something Tiger felt he could do at the time. So Mark and I showed Tiger the proper release to hit that shot. The feeling is that the back of the left hand squares and bows down at impact to take loft off the clubface and then there is a relaxing of the elbows through impact. That softening of the elbows breaks the momentum of the release and produces a lower shot. In other words, the club finishes low and the ball follows suit.

Tiger was curious, but after we showed him the shot and how Mark was playing it, his reaction was that he wasn't strong enough to do it. Of course that wasn't the case, but his perception was that to "hold off" the finish in that manner took an incredible amount of strength. Even after we explained that the key wasn't strength but technique, he still didn't believe he could do it.

Years later, early in our working relationship, I was showing Tiger that same shot in preparation for a trip to the British Open.

He got it. He knows now that the more you relax your arms and the less you use your strength, the more able you are to get that proper release for a low shot.

One more thing about the low shot: your ball position should stay the same as normal, unless you are punching out from underneath some trees and have to keep the ball extremely low. If that is the case, you can move the ball back in your stance as much as necessary to keep it down.

FIGURE 96 The more your wrists fold the club up, the higher up the shot will fly.

The High Shot

This time I need to get the ball over those branches, or the hole is cut at the front of the green and there is a bunker between the flag and me. So a high shot is called for, and I need to make a bigger and faster swing. A lot of people advocate changing the ball position for both low and high shots, but I don't like to see that too much. With the club swinging on an arc, it is square for only one brief moment—hopefully right where you hit the ball—so if you move it too far forward (or back for the low shot), you are going to have a tendency to pull the shot to the left (and push it to the right with the ball back). That gets you into the area of making compensations, a road I'd rather not see you go down.

What I do recommend is a slight change of where your body weight is emphasized at address. For this shot, get a little more of your weight on your right side at address (on your left for the low shot).

As for the release of the club for a high shot, go for a little less extension in your hands, arms, and club than you did when hitting the low shot, then relax your elbows—as you did before—but let the clubhead flow through into a higher finish, with your hands and wrists more active through the shot (figure 96). Let the length of your follow-through dictate just how high the shot goes. A longer follow-through equals a higher shot.

CONCLUSION

Get started on your plan for improvement by making a complete analysis of your golf game. Identify where and what you need to improve, especially in terms of your typical ball flight.

Where do your worst or most consistent misses finish in relation to the target?

Which shots do you find most difficult?

Which shots are easiest for you?

What does your swing look like, specifically its shape?

What does your swing feel like?

The best place to work on your fundamentals is at home. Start with your grip. Practice getting the correct feeling of your hands on the club. This is especially important if you are making a significant change to the way you hold the club.

Next, rehearse your stance, posture, and alignment while standing in front of a mirror. Make sure you check your positions and body angles both from side on and down the line. This may sound tedious or even a bit boring, but it is never a waste of time. It is amazing how things can change from day to day, so never take your setup for granted.

Once you are happy with all the stationary aspects of your pre-swing, work on your takeaway. So much of the golf swing is action and reaction, so making sure your first move into the backswing is correct will have a huge influence on what happens later.

After grooving your setup and takeaway, work through the backswing and the downswing, one step at a time. Alternate between focusing on the movement of the club as it pertains to the plane of the swing and what your body is doing as it turns and coils in the backswing then unwinds in the downswing.

Last, always take time to practice your release motion; it is so important to the resulting quality of your shots. Make little backswings in slow motion, squaring the back of your left hand as you return to the ball. If you have a correct grip and the back of your left hand faces the target at impact, then that is where the ball will go, too. Use your mirror to check that this is correct.

Next up is your throughswing, from impact all the way to the end of your follow-through. Think of it as a mirror image of your backswing. Again, focus first on what the club is doing in relation to your swing plane, then on your body motion.

Rehearsing your swing in front of a mirror is the best way to implement changes in your swing. But rehearsing your swing in your mind can be almost as valuable. Do both before you practice or play, and you will see great results.

Before you know it, you will have a fundamentally correct golf swing that is both powerful and consistent. When you have that to work with, it won't take you much longer to "own" your method. It all starts with perfecting the essentials of the swing.

Best of luck.

INDEX

Page numbers in italics refer to illustrations.